# CUTTING
# EDGE

## NEW EDITION

STARTER

STUDENTS' BOOK

WITH DVD-ROM

SARAH CUNNINGHAM PETER MOOR
CHRIS REDSTON AND ARAMINTA CRACE

# CONTENTS

| Pronunciation | Task | Language live | Study, Practice & Remember |
|---|---|---|---|
| Short forms: *am*, *is* Word stress: jobs and numbers | Ask for and give personal information **Preparation**: Listening **Task**: Speaking | **Speaking**: Saying hello and goodbye **Writing**: Write about yourself; sentences and questions | Study & Practice 1, page 98 Study & Practice 2, page 98 Study & Practice 3, page 99 Remember these words, page 99 |
| Word stress: nationalities Sounds: *His* and *He's* | Do a quiz **Preparation**: Listening and reading **Task**: Speaking | | Study & Practice 1, page 100 Study & Practice 2, page 100 Remember these words, page 101 |
| Sounds: *th* Word stress: adjectives | Talk about your favourite food **Preparation**: Listening **Task**: Speaking | **Speaking**: In a café **Writing**: Holiday messages | Study & Practice 1, page 102 Study & Practice 2, page 102 Remember these words, page 103 |
| Word stress: places and natural features Sounds: *th* | Talk about your home town **Preparation**: Listening **Task**: Speaking | **Speaking**: Asking for directions **Writing**: Your town | Study & Practice 1, page 104 Study & Practice 2, page 104 Study & Practice 3, page 105 Remember these words, page 105 |
| Word stress: family words Sounds: possessive *'s* | Present your personal profile **Preparation**: Listening **Task**: Speaking | | Study & Practice 1, page 106 Study & Practice 2, page 106 Study & Practice 3, page 106 Remember these words, page 107 |
| Sounds: present simple verb endings with *'s* and *-es* Linking: *Does he* and *Does she* | Giving information about someone **Preparation**: Listening **Task**: Speaking | **Speaking**: Making offers **Writing**: Your classmate; *and* and *but* | Study & Practice 1, page 108 Study & Practice 2, page 108 Remember these words, page 109 |

# CONTENTS

# 01

# NICE TO MEET YOU

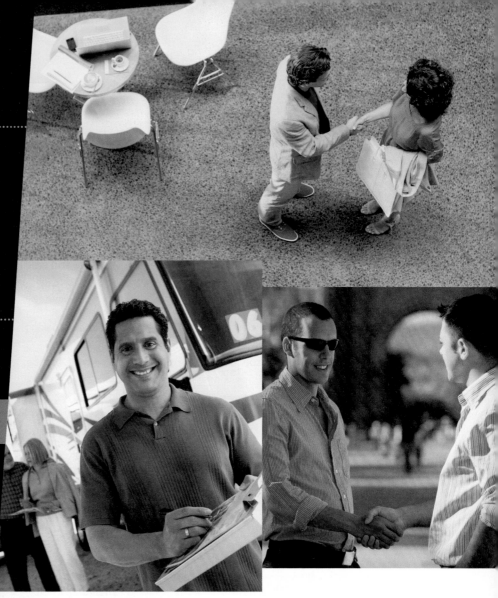

## IN THIS UNIT

- Grammar: *I* and *you* (*I'm ... / Are you ...?*); *my* and *your* (*What's your name? / My name's ...*); *a/an* with jobs (*I'm a student. / Are you an actor?*)
- Vocabulary: Jobs; The alphabet / *How do you spell ...?*; Numbers 0–20 / *What's your phone number?*
- Task: Ask for and give personal information
- Language live: Saying hello and goodbye; S entences and questions

## Grammar focus 1
### Names and introductions: *I* and *you*; *my* and *your*

1  🎧 1.1 Listen to the conversations. Practise saying them.

   1  **A:** Hello, my name's Daniel.
      **B:** Hi, Daniel. I'm Eva. Nice to meet you.
   2  **A:** Hello, I'm Ben.
   3  **A:** Hi, I'm Tim.
      **B:** Hello, my name's Sam. Nice to meet you.

2a Complete the conversations with *I* and *my*.

   1  **A:** Hi, ¹ _____ 'm Kate.
      **B:** Hello, Kate. ² _____ name's James. Nice to meet you.
   2  **A:** Hello, ³ _____ name's Tom.
      **B:** Hi, Tom. ⁴ _____ 'm Juliet. Nice to meet you.
   3  **A:** Hello, ⁵ _____ name's Steve.
      **B:** Hello, Steve. ⁶ _____ name's Kara. Nice to meet you.

   b  🎧 1.2 Listen and check.

**I**'m Vicky. ( = I am)
**My** name's Vicky. (= name is)
Are **you** Sam?
What's **your** name? (= what is)

**4a** Choose the correct words.

    **1** Hello, **I** / **You** 'm Daniel.
    **2** Are **I** / **you** Tom?
    **3** Hi. Are **I** / **you** Sarah?
    **4** **I** / **You** 'm Anton.
    **5** Hello, **my** / **your** name's Kate.
    **6** What's **my** / **your** name?
    **7** **My** / **Your** name's Masumi.
    **8** Hi. What's **my** / **your** name?

**b** 🎧 1.4 **Listen and check.**

**PRONUNCIATION**

**1** Listen again to sentences 5–8 in exercise 4.

**2** Practise saying the sentences.

**3** 🎧 1.3 **Look at the pictures and listen.**

What's your name?

My name's Amelia.

Are you Mike Wilson?

Yes, that's right.

**5a** Complete the conversations with *I*, *my*, *you* or *your*.

    **1** **A:** Hello, _____ name's Harry.
        **B:** Hi, Harry. _____ 'm Sandra. Nice to meet you.
    **2** **A:** Are _____ Michael?
        **B:** Yes, that's right.
    **3** **A:** What's _____ name?
        **B:** _____ name's Simon Dodds.
    **4** **A:** Hi, _____ 'm Julia.
        **B:** Hello, Julia. _____ name's Jenny.
    **5** **A:** Are _____ Kim Watson?
        **B:** No, _____ 'm Kim Watts.
    **6** **A:** What's _____ name?
        **B:** _____ name's Mike.

**b** 🎧 1.5 **Listen and check.**

**6** Practise the conversations with other students. Use your names.

Are you Harry?

No, I'm Hugo.

Hello, my name's Alex.

Hi, Alex. I'm Carla. Nice to meet you.

**Unit 1, Study & Practice 1, page 98**

## Vocabulary
### Jobs

**1** 🎧 1.6 **Look at the photos. Listen and say the jobs.**

waiter/waitress      businessman/businesswoman
engineer      actor
teacher      police officer
accountant      shop assistant

---

### PRONUNCIATION

**1** Listen again to the jobs in exercise 1. Mark the stress.
tea•cher      wai•ter

**2** Listen again and practise saying the jobs.

---

## Grammar focus 2
### a/an with jobs

**1** 🎧 1.7 **Listen and complete the sentences.**

1 My name's Antonia. I'm a _____ .
2 Hello, I'm Denise. I'm a _____ .
3 Hi, I'm Joshua. I'm a _____ .
4 My name's Bradley. I'm an _____ .
5 Hello, my name's Tina. I'm a _____ .
6 My name's Lewis. I'm an _____ .
7 Hi, I'm Karis. I'm a _____ .
8 Hello, my name's Jake. I'm an _____ .

---

### GRAMMAR

*a/an* with jobs

| *an* + vowel (*a, e, i, o, u*) | I'm **an a**ctor. <br> I'm **an e**ngineer. |
|---|---|
| *a* + consonant (*b, c, d, f,* ...) | I'm **a b**usinesswoman. <br> I'm **a t**eacher. |

**2** Write the jobs in exercise 1 in the correct place.

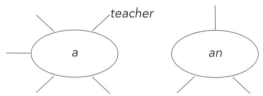

*teacher*

a                 an

**3a** Complete the conversations with *a* or *an*.

1 **A:** What's your job?
  **B:** I'm _____ teacher.
2 **A:** Are you _____ engineer?
  **B:** No, I'm _____ architect.
3 **A:** Are you _____ shop assistant?
  **B:** Yes, that's right.
4 **A:** Are you _____ student?
  **B:** No, I'm _____ accountant.

**b** 🎧 1.8 **Listen and check.**

**4** Practise the conversations with other students. Change the jobs.

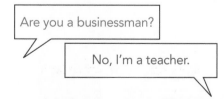

Are you a businessman?

No, I'm a teacher.

---

Unit 1, Study & Practice 2, page 98

## Vocabulary
### The alphabet and *How do you spell ...?*

1 🎧 1.9 Listen and say the alphabet.

# Aa Bb Cc Dd Ee Ff Gg Hh Ii Jj *Kk* Ll Mm Nn Oo Pp Qq Rr Ss Tt *Uu* Vv Ww Xx *Yy* Zz

| Airport code | | |
|---|---|---|
| 1 _ _ _ | Dubai International Airport, UAE | |
| 2 _ _ _ | John F. Kennedy Airport, New York, USA | |
| 3 _ _ _ | Zürich Airport, Switzerland | |
| 4 _ _ _ | Narita Airport, Tokyo, Japan | |
| 5 _ _ _ | Los Angeles International Airport, USA | |
| 6 _ _ _ | Vancouver International Airport, Canada | |
| 7 _ _ _ | London Gatwick Airport, UK | |
| 8 _ _ _ | Atatürk International Airport, Istanbul, Turkey | |
| 9 _ _ _ | Galeão International Airport, Rio de Janeiro, Brazil | |
| 10 _ _ _ | Beijing Capital International Airport, China | |

2a 🎧 1.10 Listen and choose the correct answers.

1 LAX / LEX
2 YVR / WVR
3 EST / IST
4 DXB / DSB
5 MRT / NRT
6 BEK / PEK
7 ZAH / ZRH
8 LGW / LJW
9 JFK / GFK
10 GEG / GIG

**IT'S A FACT!**
There are 26 letters in the English alphabet.

b 🎧 1.11 Listen and write the airport codes in the table.

c Work in pairs and say the airport codes.

3a 🎧 1.12 Work in pairs. Listen and spell the words.

*How do you spell 'Dubai'?*
*D-U-B-A-I*

b Work in pairs. Choose three more places and ask your partner, '*How do you spell ...?*'.

*How do you spell 'Beijing'?*
*B-E-I-J-I-N-G*

4 Work in pairs. Ask questions with '*How do you spell ...?*' using the ideas in the box.

your first name                     your surname
your teacher's surname              the name of your town
the name of your school/workplace

How do you spell your first name?

V-A-N-E-S-S-A

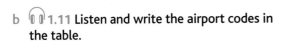

Unit 1, Study & Practice 3, page 99

## Vocabulary
### Numbers 0–20

1a 🎧 1.13 Listen and say the numbers.

| | | | | | |
|---|---|---|---|---|---|
| **1** | **one** | **5** | **five** | **9** | **nine** |
| **2** | **two** | **6** | **six** | **10** | **ten** |
| **3** | **three** | **7** | **seven** | **11** | **eleven** |
| **4** | **four** | **8** | **eight** | **12** | **twelve** |

b 🎧 1.14 Listen and write the numbers you hear.

c Write the numbers from exercise 1b in words.

2 Work in pairs. Write a number (0–12). Your partner says the number.

3a 🎧 1.15 Listen and say the numbers.

| | | | |
|---|---|---|---|
| **13** | **thirteen** | **17** | **seventeen** |
| **14** | **fourteen** | **18** | **eighteen** |
| **15** | **fifteen** | **19** | **nineteen** |
| **16** | **sixteen** | **20** | **twenty** |

b 🎧 1.16 Listen and write the numbers you hear.

### PRONUNCIATION

1 🎧 1.17 Listen and mark the stress on numbers 0–20.
zero, one,

2 Listen again and practise saying the numbers.

4a 🎧 1.18 Listen to the conversations and complete the phone numbers.

**Conversation 1**
A: What's your phone number?
B: My phone number's 0134 ___ 45 ___ 22 ___ .

**Conversation 2**
A: What's your phone number?
B: It's 0775 ___ 909 _____ .

**Conversation 3**
A: What's your phone number?
B: My phone number is 07 _____ 887 _____ .

b Work in pairs. Listen again and repeat the conversations. Then practise using different phone numbers.

# Task

## Ask for and give personal information

### Preparation Listening

1 🎧 1.19 Listen to four conversations. Tick the information they give.

- first name
- email address
- job
- phone number
- surname

2 Listen again and complete the information.

**A**

| First name | Irina |
|---|---|
| Surname | ¹_____ |
| Phone number | 07789 223433 |
| Email address | tara12@global.com |

**B**

| First name | James |
|---|---|
| Surname | White |
| Phone number | ²_____ |
| Email address | white.j20@ tmail.com |

**C**

| First name | Barbara |
|---|---|
| Surname | ³_____ |
| Phone number | 07404 772698 |
| Email address | ⁴_____ |

**D**

| First name | Yasir |
|---|---|
| Surname | ⁵_____ |
| Phone number | ⁶_____ |
| Email address | yasir15@newmail.com |

3 Listen again and tick the phrases you hear in the Useful language box (a and b).

# Task Speaking

**1a** Match the questions in the Useful language box with the headings below.

- First name  • Surname  • Phone number  • Email address

**b** Write answers to the questions using your personal information.

**2** Ask three students questions about their personal information and complete the tables below.

> Useful language a and b

**A**

| First name | |
|---|---|
| Surname | |
| Phone number | |
| Email address | |

**B**

| First name | |
|---|---|
| Surname | |
| Phone number | |
| Email address | |

**C**

| First name | |
|---|---|
| Surname | |
| Phone number | |
| Email address | |

**3** Work in pairs and take turns to give your personal information.

*My first name's Eddie and my surname's Alessi.*
*My phone number is …*

### SHARE YOUR TASK

Practise saying your personal information.

Film/Record yourself saying your personal information.

Share your film/recording with other students.

11

# LANGUAGE LIVE

Hello

Nice to meet you

## Speaking
### Saying hello and goodbye

**1**  Watch the video and tick the phrases you hear.

1 How are you?
2 Hi, I'm Mark.
3 Nice to meet you.
4 What's your name?
5 How do you spell it?
6 This is Andrew.
7 Goodbye! See you again!

**2** Watch again and match the sentence pairs.

1 How are you?
2 Hi, I'm Mark.
3 Nice to meet you.
4 What's your name?
5 How do you spell it?
6 This is Andrew.
7 Goodbye, Mark. See you again!

a Hello, Mark.
b Hello, Andrew.
c I'm fine. How are you?
d Goodbye. See you again!
e My name's ...
f Nice to meet you.
g S-I-...

## PRONUNCIATION

**1** ▶ Watch and listen to the key phrases.

**2** Practise saying them.

**3** Choose the correct answer (a, b or c).

1 How are you?
  a I'm fine.
  b My name's John.
  c Nice to meet you.
2 What's your name?
  a Hello, Kate.
  b My name's Jo.
  c See you again.
3 How do you spell your name?
  a L-I-A.
  b My name's Lia.
  c Nice to meet you.

**4a** Complete the conversations.

...................................................................
fine   Hi   name   Nice   This   See   spell
...................................................................

1 A: How are you ?
  B: I'm _____ . How are you?
2 A: _____ ! I'm Simon.
  B: _____ to meet you, Simon.
3 A: What's your _____ ?
  B: My name's Kara.
  A: How do you _____ it?
4 A: _____ is Adam.
  B: Hello, Adam.
5 A: Goodbye, Paola. _____ you again!
  B: Goodbye!

**b** Work in pairs and practise the conversations.
Use your own names.

# Writing
## Sentences and questions

**1** Circle the full stops and underline the question marks in the conversation.

**A:** Hello. What's your name?
**B:** My name's Jan.
**A:** How do you spell it?
**B:** J-A-N.
**A:** Hello, Jan.

**2a** Read the information about full stops and question marks.

- We use a full stop (.) at the end of a sentence.
*Nice to meet you.*

- We use a question mark (?) at the end of a question.
*How are you?*

**b** Tick the correct sentences and cross the incorrect sentences.

What's your name. **x**
What's your name? **✓**
1 **a** My name's Tom.
  **b** My name's Tom?
2 **a** Are you Frida Jonsson.
  **b** Are you Frida Jonsson?
3 **a** No, I'm Maria Jonsson.
  **b** No, I'm Maria Jonsson?
4 **a** How do you spell your name?
  **b** How do you spell your name.

**3** Complete the conversations with full stops and question marks.

1 **A:** Are you Jo White ___
  **B:** Yes ___
  **A:** Hello ___ I'm Paul Gray ___
  **B:** Nice to meet you ___
2 **A:** How are you ___
  **B:** I'm fine ___ How are you ___
  **A:** I'm OK ___
3 **A:** My name's Helen ___
  **B:** What's your email address ___
  **A:** It's *helendesanto@bp.com* ___
  **B:** How do you spell it ___

**4a** Read the information about capital letters.

We use capital letters:
- with names.
*David Williams    Julia Kay*

- at the beginning of a sentence.
*Hello, my name's Michael.*
*Nice to meet you!*

**b** Write capital letters in the correct places.

1 my name's andrew.
2 are you a teacher?
3 My name is tom woods. i'm an actor.
4 hello, tom. nice to meet you.
5 how do you spell your first name?
6 i'm anna. i'm a student.
7 are you david?
8 what's your name?

**5a** Complete the information with the words in the box.

a   email address   is   my   name   phone number

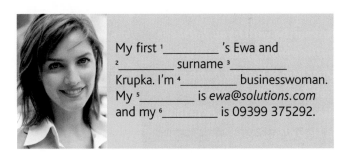

My first ¹_____ 's Ewa and
²_____ surname ³_____
Krupka. I'm ⁴_____ businesswoman.
My ⁵_____ is *ewa@solutions.com*
and my ⁶_____ is 09399 375292.

**b** Complete the table with information about Ewa and then with information about you.

|  | Ewa | you |
|---|---|---|
| first name |  |  |
| surname |  |  |
| job |  |  |
| email address |  |  |
| phone number |  |  |

**6** Write a paragraph about you. Use the example in exercise 5a to help you. Use capital letters where necessary.

# 02

## AROUND THE WORLD

### IN THIS UNIT

- Grammar: *be* with *I, you, he/she/it* (*She/He's from ...*); *his/her* (*What's his/her name? His/Her name's ...*)
- Vocabulary: Countries and nationalities; Numbers (21–100) and *How old ...?*
- Task: Do a quiz

## Vocabulary
### Countries

1a 🎧 **2.1** Listen and say the countries.

| | | | | |
|---|---|---|---|---|
| Australia | Brazil | China | Egypt | England |
| Italy | Japan | Russia | the USA | Vietnam |

b Which of the countries in the box can you see in the photos?

2 Work in pairs. Write the name of:

1 your country.
2 a country near your country.
3 a country with the same language as your country.

## Grammar focus 1
### *be* with *I* and *you*

1 🎧 **2.2** Listen to two conversations. Number the sentences in the order you hear them.

**Conversation 1**
No, I'm not.
Are you from Brazil? *1*
I'm from Italy.
Oh. Where are you from?

**Conversation 2**
Where are you from?
The USA? No, I'm not.
I'm from England.
Are you from the USA? *1*

## GRAMMAR

*be* with *I* and *you*

| + | **I'm** from Russia. (= I am) <br> **You're** from Australia. (= you are) |
|---|---|
| – | **I'm not** from Italy. (= I am) <br> **You aren't** from Egypt. (= are not) |
| ? | Where **are you** from? <br> **Are you** from Spain? Yes, **I am**. / No, **I'm not**. |

**2a** 🎧 **2.3** Complete the conversation. Listen and check.

| are | I | 'm | not | you |
|---|---|---|---|---|

A: Where ¹_____ you from?
B: I ²_____ from Australia. And you?
A: ³_____ 'm from Italy.
B: Really? Are ⁴_____ from Rome?
A: No, I'm ⁵_____ . I'm from Milan.

**b** Practise saying the conversation. Use different countries and cities.

# Grammar focus 2

## *be* with *he*, *she* and *it*

Daniel Day Lewis is an actor. He's from London in England. Rebecca Miller is a director. She's from Connecticut in the USA.

**1a** Read the information.

**b** 🎧 **2.4** Match questions 1–5 with answers a–e. Listen and check.

1 Is Daniel Day Lewis a director?
2 Is he from England?
3 Is London in the USA?
4 Is Rebecca Miller from England?
5 Where's Connecticut?

a Yes, he is.
b No, he isn't. He's an actor.
c No, she isn't. She's from the USA.
d It's in the USA.
e No, it isn't. It's in England.

## GRAMMAR

*be* with *he*, *she* and *it*

| + | **He's** from England. (= he is) <br> **It's** in the USA. (= it is) |
|---|---|
| – | **She isn't** from England. (= is not) <br> **It isn't** in Australia. (= is not) |
| ? | Where**'s she** from? (= is she) <br> **Is he** from Russia? Yes, **he is**. / No, **he isn't**. (= is not) |

**2** 🎧 **2.5** Complete the conversations with *is*, *'s* or *isn't*. Listen and check.

1 A: _____ your teacher from Australia?
   B: No, she _____ .
2 A: Where _____ Nawal El Saadawi from?
   B: She _____ from Egypt.
3 A: _____ Barack Obama from the USA?
   B: Yes, he _____ .
4 A: _____ your best friend from Russia?
   B: No, he _____ .
5 A: Where _____ Dilma Rousseff from?
   B: I don't know.

Stephanie Rice

Vladimir Putin

Lang Lang

Neymar

Adele

Oprah Winfrey

**3** Work in pairs. Look at the people in the photos. Ask and answer questions about them. Use the countries in the box.

Australia  Brazil  China  England  Russia  the USA

> Where is Stephanie Rice from?
>> She's from Australia.

Unit 2, Study & Practice 1, page 100

| A | Argentina | Australia | Egypt | Japan |
|---|-----------|-----------|-------|-------|
|   | Poland    | Portugal  | Spain | the USA |

| B | Polish   | Portuguese  | Australian | Spanish |
|---|----------|-------------|------------|---------|
|   | American | Argentinian | Japanese   | Egyptian |

b Complete the table in exercise 1b with the countries and nationalities in exercise 2a.

---

## PRONUNCIATION

1 🎧 2.7 Listen to the nationalities in exercise 1b. Mark the stress.

Rússian        Ameŕican

2 Practise saying the nationalities.

---

3 Complete the conversations with the correct nationalities.

1 **A:** Is Marco from Portugal?
  **B:** Yes, he's _____ .
2 **A:** Is Sara from Egypt?
  **B:** Yes, she's _____ .
3 **A:** Is Marek from Poland?
  **B:** Yes, he's _____ .
4 **A:** Is Marina from Argentina?
  **B:** Yes, she's _____ .
5 **A:** Is Chen from China?
  **B:** Yes, he's _____ .
6 **A:** Is Sylvie from Spain?
  **B:** Yes, she's _____ .

4 Work in pairs. Practise similar conversations with the names and nationalities below or your own ideas.

- Gustavo / Brazil
- Jane / Australia
- Marek / Poland
- Ali / Egypt
- Adriana / Spain
- Akiko / Japan

> Is Gustavo from Brazil?
>> Yes, he's Brazilian.

**IT'S A FACT!**
400,000 Australian people are in Britain and 1.3 million British people are in Australia.

---

# Vocabulary
## Countries and nationalities

1a 🎧 2.6 Look at the photos. Read and listen to the information about the people.

1 My name's Feng. I'm from Shanghai in China. I'm Chinese.
2 I'm Sofiya. I'm from Moscow in Russia. I'm Russian.
3 I'm Thiago. I'm from Rio de Janeiro in Brazil. I'm Brazilian.
4 My name's Ellie. I'm from Manchester in England. I'm English.

b Write the nationalities from exercise 1a in the table (1–4).

|   | Country | Nationality | Ending |
|---|---------|-------------|--------|
| A | Russia  | ¹_____     | + -n   |
|   | _____  | _____      |        |
|   | _____  | _____      |        |
| B | China   | ²_____     | + -ese |
|   | _____  | _____      |        |
|   | _____  | _____      |        |
| C | Brazil  | ³_____     | + -ian |
|   | _____  | _____      |        |
|   | _____  | _____      |        |
| D | England | ⁴_____     | + -ish |
|   | _____  | _____      |        |
|   | _____  | _____      |        |

Oksana Domnina, Maxim Shabalin

Javier Bardem

Jessie J

# Grammar focus 3
## his/her

**1** 🎧 2.8 **Look at the photos. Listen and complete the nationalities.**

**1** His name's Javier Bardem and he's _____ .
**2** Her name's Jessie J and she's _____ .
**3** Her name's Oksana Domnina and she's _____ .
His name's Maxim Shabalin and he's _____ , too.

**GRAMMAR**

*his/her*

| his | What's **his** name? **His** name's Maxim.<br>Is **his** name Maxim? Yes, it is. / No, it isn't.<br><br>**Notice:**<br>Where's **he** from? **He**'s from England. |
|-----|---|
| her | What's **her** name? **Her** name's Sandra.<br>Is **her** name Oksana? Yes, it is. / No, it isn't.<br><br>**Notice:**<br>Where's **she** from? **She**'s from Russia. |

**2** 🎧 2.9 **Complete the conversations with** *his*, *her*, *he* **or** *she*. **Listen and check.**

**1** **A:** What's her name?
   **B:** _____ name's Marianna.
**2** **A:** Where's he from?
   **B:** He's from Egypt. _____ 's Egyptian.
**3** **A:** Is his name Antonio?
   **B:** No, it isn't. _____ name's Anton.
**4** **A:** Where's she from?
   **B:** She's from Japan. _____ 's Japanese.
**5** **A:** What's _____ job?
   **B:** He's a teacher.
**6** **A:** Where's she from?
   **B:** She's from Spain. _____ 's Spanish.

Lionel Messi

Vanessa Amorosi

Sandra Bullock

**3** **Work in pairs. Match the people in the photos above with what they do.**

**1** Sandra Bullock          **a** Argentinian footballer
**2** Lionel Messi            **b** Australian singer
**3** Vanessa Amorosi         **c** American actor

**4a** **Complete the conversation with information about Sandra Bullock. Write full sentences.**

**A:** What's her name?
**B:** _____ .
**A:** Where's she from?
**B:** _____ .
**A:** What's her job?
**B:** _____ .

**b** **Work in pairs. Practise similar conversations about Lionel Messi, Vanessa Amorosi and other people in the photos on this page.**

What's his name?

His name's Lionel Messi.

**Unit 2, Study & Practice 2, page 100**

## Vocabulary
### Numbers (21–100) and *How old ...?*

1  🎧 2.12 Listen and say the numbers.

| | |
|---|---|
| **20 twenty** | **70 seventy** |
| **30 thirty** | **80 eighty** |
| **40 forty** | **90 ninety** |
| **50 fifty** | **100 a hundred** |
| **60 sixty** | |

2a  Write the numbers as words.

| | |
|---|---|
| **20 twenty** | **25** _____ |
| **21 twenty-one** | **26** _____ |
| **22 twenty-two** | **27** _____ |
| **23** _____ | **28** _____ |
| **24** _____ | **29 twenty-nine** |

b  🎧 2.13 Listen and check. Practise saying the numbers.

3  🎧 2.14 Listen and write the numbers you hear. Then write them as words.

4  Work in pairs and take turns. Say the numbers from 20–29, 30–39, 40–49, 50–59, etc.

5a  Work in pairs and look at the photos. How old is each person?

Ben

Eva

Tim

b  🎧 2.15 Listen and write the age of each person.

6  Work in pairs. Look at the photos of people in Units 1 and 2. Ask and answer questions about their ages.

> How old is Javier Bardem?

> I think he's forty.

> Really? I think he's fifty ...

# Task

## Do a quiz

## Preparation  Listening and reading

1a  Work in pairs and look at the photos. Who or what are they?

b  Look at the names in **bold** in the quiz and check your answers.

2a  🎧 2.16 Listen to two people doing the first part of the quiz. Tick the questions they talk about.

b  Listen again and tick the questions and answers you hear in the Useful language box (a and b).

## People, places, companies ... an international quiz

**1 Hugh Jackman** is an actor. Is he:
a British?    b American?   c Australian?

**2 Where is the River Amazon?**
a Argentina   b Brazil      c the USA

**3 Zara** is a clothes company. Is it:
a Spanish?    b Russian?    c Portuguese?

**4 Where is the Great Pyramid of Giza?**
a China       b Egypt       c Russia

**5 Alisher Usmanov** is a businessman.
**Where is he from?**
a Poland      b the USA     c Russia

**6 Where is The Shard?**
a Dubai       b London      c New York

**7 Toyota** is a car company. Is it:
a Chinese?    b Japanese?   c American?

**8 Claudia Leitte** is a singer. Is she:
a English?    b Brazilian?  c Argentinian?

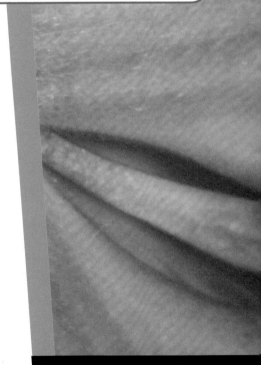

## USEFUL LANGUAGE

**a Questions**
Where's he/she from?
Where's it from?
Where is it?
What's his/her name?
What's his/her job?

**b Answers**
I think he's/she's (American/Australian).
He/She isn't (British/American).
He's/She's from (Britain/Argentina).
He/She isn't from (Japan/Egypt).
I think it's in (Brazil/Japan).
It isn't in (Britain/Argentina).
It's a (Japanese/Spanish) company.
I don't know.

## Task Speaking

1   Work in pairs and do the quiz. Use the questions and answers in the Useful language box.

> Useful language a and b

2   Read the information on page 96 and check your answers.

3   Work in pairs. Choose six people, places or companies from the quiz. Practise saying the information about them.

## SHARE YOUR TASK

**Practise saying information about six people, places or companies from the quiz.**

**Film/record yourself saying the information.**

**Share your film/recording with other students.**

# 03

# GOING PLACES

## IN THIS UNIT

- Grammar: *this/that, these/those*; *be* with *we* and *they*
- Vocabulary: Plural nouns; Adjectives–opposites; Food and drink
- Task: Talk about your favourite food
- Language live: In a café; Holiday messages

## Vocabulary
### Plural nouns

1 Look at the photos. Which things in the box can you see?

taxi/taxis    car/cars         bus/buses        shop/shops      city/cities
man/men       woman/women      person/people    child/children

2 Match the singular nouns in A with the plural nouns in B.

| A | B |
|---|---|
| 1 a student | a sandwiches |
| 2 an address | b addresses |
| 3 a country | c countries |
| 4 a sandwich | d places |
| 5 a nationality | e nationalities |
| 6 a place | f students |

### PRONUNCIATION

1 🎧 3.1 Listen to the plural nouns in exercises 1 and 2.

2 Practise saying them.

3 Work in pairs and take turns. Student A say a singular noun from exercise 1 or 2. Student B say a number and the plural noun.

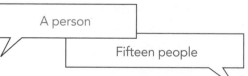

A person

Fifteen people

## GRAMMAR

*this/that, these/those*

| Singular | **this** sandwich, **this** car<br>**that** shop, **that** bus |
|----------|---------------------------------------------|
| Plural | **these** children, **these** people<br>**those** taxis, **those** countries |

**2a** Choose the correct answers.

1 What's the name of *that / those* shop?
2 *This / These* people are Spanish.
3 Who are *that / those* children?
4 Look at *this / these* place!
5 Is *that / those* your bus?
6 *This / These* students are my friends.
7 Who are *that / those* women?
8 *This / These* country is beautiful!

**b** 🎧 3.3 Listen and check.

## PRONUNCIATION

1 Listen again to the sentences in exercise 2a. Notice the pronunciation of *th-* in *this, that, these* and *those*.

2 Practise saying *this, that, these* and *those*.

**3** 🎧 3.4 Complete the conversations with *this, that, these* and *those*. Listen and check.

**A:** Who's ¹_____ man?
**B:** He's my teacher.

**A:** Alex, ²_____ is James.
**B:** Hello, James.

**A:** Where are ³_____ people from?
**B:** They're from Italy.

**A:** ⁴_____ two books, please.
**B:** £10, please.

**4** Work in pairs and practise the conversations in exercises 1 and 3.

Unit 3, Study & Practice 1, page 102

# Grammar focus 1
*this/that, these/those*

**1** 🎧 3.2 Listen to the conversations and choose the correct answers.

**A:** What's ¹*this / that*?
**B:** It's a sandwich!

**A:** Look at ²*this / that* shop!
**B:** Yes, it's fantastic!

**A:** Are ³*these / those* taxis?
**B:** Yes, let's go!

**A:** ⁴*These / Those* are my children, Jim and Alice.
**B:** Hello!

**Amanda Foster**
We're in New York! The people here are friendly and our hotel is in the city centre. It's fantastic!
12 people like this ✓

..................................................

**Comments**
**Jack Rose** Is the hotel expensive?
**Amanda Foster** No, it isn't. It's really cheap.
**Jack Rose** What about the restaurants? Are they expensive?
**Amanda Foster** No! The restaurants aren't expensive either! They're really good … . Italian food, Chinese food, Japanese food … . everything!
**Nicola Jameson** What about things to do?
**Amanda Foster** Lots of things to do … . parks, shops, restaurants, museums! New York is one of my favourite cities. It's a fantastic holiday and we're all very happy! ☺

# Reading and vocabulary
## Common adjectives

**1** Look at the photos and read the text.

   **1** Where are they?
   **2** Are they on holiday or on business?

**2a** 🎧 **3.5** Look at the pictures below. Listen and repeat the adjectives

friendly    unfriendly
cheap    expensive
happy    sad
fantastic    awful

**b** Read the text in exercise 1 again and choose the correct adjectives .

   **1** The people are *friendly* / *unfriendly*.
   **2** The hotel is *cheap* / *expensive*.
   **3** We are *happy* / *sad*.
   **4** The holiday is *fantastic* / *awful*.

**c** 🎧 **3.6** Listen and check your answers.

**3** Choose the correct answers.

   **1** The people are *friendly* / *expensive*.
   **2** That hotel is *happy* / *cheap*.
   **3** The holiday is *fantastic* / *sad*.
   **4** That shop is *expensive* / *happy*.
   **5** The waiter is *cheap* / *unfriendly*.
   **6** That man is *sad* / *cheap*.

**4a** Complete the sentences using the adjectives in exercise 2a.

   **1** Today I am _____ .
   **2** The people at my school/work are _____ .
   **3** The waiters in my favourite restaurant are _____ .
   **4** My city is _____ .
   **5** Buses in my city are _____ .
   **6** People in my country are _____ .

**b** Work in pairs and compare your sentences.

# Grammar focus 2
## *be* with *we* and *they*

**1** Choose the correct answers. Look at the text in exercise 1 on page 22 to help you.

1 We *is* / *are* all very happy.
2 The people here *is* / *are* friendly.
3 The hotel *isn't* / *aren't* expensive.
4 The restaurants *isn't* / *aren't* expensive.

### GRAMMAR

*be* with *we* and *they*

| + | **We're** in New York. (= we are)<br>**They're** expensive. (= they are) |
|---|---|
| – | **We aren't** in New York. (= are not)<br>**They aren't** expensive. (= are not) |
| ? | **Are we** in New York?<br>**Are they** expensive? |

Remember:  **He's** in New York.   **It isn't** expensive.

**2a** Choose the correct answers.

My name's Joana and I'm from Kraków in Poland. My friends Giulia and Massimo ¹*is* / *are* also students. They ²*isn't* / *aren't* from Poland – they ³*is* / *are* from Italy. We ⁴*is* / *are* in Boston now – we ⁵*is* / *are* students at the university. Our flat ⁶*is* / *are* very expensive, but the shops ⁷*isn't* / *aren't* expensive. The people ⁸*is* / *are* very friendly – Boston ⁹*is* / *are* a fantastic city!

b **3.8 Listen and check.**

Sumiko and I ¹_____ from Tokyo in Japan and we ²_____ engineers. We ³_____ in Japan now – we ⁴_____ in Sydney in Australia for a conference. Alex and Kim ⁵_____ also engineers. They ⁶_____ from Japan – they ⁷_____ from Brazil. Sydney ⁸_____ a great city and the conference ⁹_____ fantastic. But the restaurant in the hotel ¹⁰_____ good – the food ¹¹_____ awful and the waiters ¹²_____ unfriendly.

**3a** Complete the text with *is*, *isn't*, *are* or *aren't*.

b 🎧3.9 **Listen and check.**

**4a** Write four sentences about the groups of people on pages 22 and 23. Don't write their names.

*They're on holiday.*

*They're from Brazil.*

b Work in pairs and take turns. Read your sentences to your partner. Your partner says who the people are.

> They're on holiday.
>
> Amanda Foster and her family are on holiday.

IT'S A FACT!
There are approximately 47 million people on holiday in New York every year.

**Unit 3, Study & Practice 2, page 102**

## Listening and vocabulary
### Food and drink

**1a** 🎧 **3.10** Look at the pictures. Listen and repeat the words.

| | | | | | |
|---|---|---|---|---|---|
| apples | bread | cheese | chicken | coffee | eggs |
| milk | pasta | potatoes | rice | tea | water |

**b** Write the words from 1a in the correct place.

**1** Drink: _tea_, _____ , _____ , _____
**2** Meat and fish: _____
**3** Fruit: _____
**4** Vegetables: _____
**5** Other food: _bread_, _____ , _____ , _____ , _____

**c** 🎧 **3.11** Listen and check. Practise saying the words.

**2a** Look again at the food and drink in exercise 1a. Write 1, 2 or 3 next to each item.

**1** = horrible    **2** = OK    **3** = delicious

**b** Work in pairs and compare your ideas.

> I think coffee is delicious!
>
> Me too!

**3a** 🎧 **3.12** Listen to three people talking about their breakfast and complete the table.

| | Food | Drink |
|---|---|---|
| Jim, USA | | black coffee (no milk) |
| Kumiko, Japan | rice with fish | |
| Tomas, Poland | | |

**b** Discuss what is a typical breakfast for you.

# Task
## Talk about your favourite food

## Preparation Listening

**1** Work in pairs. Which food and drink can you see in the photos?

| | | | |
|---|---|---|---|
| rice | vegetables | chicken | bread |
| pasta | coffee | milk | cheese |
| ice cream | tea | orange | banana |
| apple | fish | tomato | potatoes |

**2a** 🎧 **3.13** Listen to two people, Rob and Barbara, talking about their favourite food and drink. Complete the table below.

| | Rob | Barbara |
|---|---|---|
| Nationality | English | Italian |
| Favourite food | | |
| Favourite fruit or vegetable | | |
| Favourite drink | | |

**b** Listen again and tick the questions and answers you hear in the Useful language box (a and b).

USEFUL LANGUAGE

**a Questions**
What's your favourite food?
What's your favourite fruit or vegetable?
What's your favourite drink?
What's a typical drink in (Italy)?
What about you?

**b Answers**
My favourite food is (Japanese food).
My favourite food isn't (English).
Japanese food is my favourite.
Pasta is very popular in Italy.
Tea is a popular drink in England.
My favourite drink is coffee, I think.

# Task Speaking

**1a** Complete the first column of the table with information about you. Ask your teacher for any words/phrases you need.

|  | You | Your partner |
| --- | --- | --- |
| **Favourite food** |  |  |
| **Favourite fruit or vegetable** |  |  |
| **Favourite drink** |  |  |

**b** Work in pairs and take turns. Ask your partner questions and complete the table. Use the questions and answers in the Useful language box to help you.

> Useful language a and b

**2** Tell the class about you and your partner.

> My name's Marta. My favourite food is pasta.
> Her name is Jo. Her favourite food is chicken.

**SHARE YOUR TASK**

Practise talking about your favourite food and drink.

Film/record yourself talking about your favourite food and drink.

Share your film/recording with other students.

Anything else?

## Speaking
### In a café

**1** ▶ Watch the video and choose the correct answers.

1 The man and the woman are **at home** / **on holiday**.
2 It is **breakfast time** / **lunchtime**.
3 To eat, the couple order **something different** / **the same thing**.
4 To drink, the couple order **something different** / **the same thing**.

**2** Watch again. Write P (Peter) or M (Mary) next to the food and drink they order.

| Food | Drink |
|---|---|
| • cheese | • apple juice |
| • eggs | • coffee (black) |
| • fish | • coffee (with milk) |
| • fruit | • orange juice |
| • sandwich | • tea (black) |
| • toast | • tea (with milk) |
| | • water |

**3a** Who says these phrases? Write P (Peter), M (Mary) or W (Waiter).

Yes, please?  *W*
1 For you, madam?
2 What's this?
3 Eggs for me, please.
4 The same for me, please.
5 And to drink, madam?
6 Can I have coffee, please? Black coffee.
7 Can I have tea, please? With milk.
8 Anything else?
9 Nothing for me.
10 Can I have the bill, please.

**b** Watch again and check your answers.

### PRONUNCIATION

1 ▶ Watch and listen to the key phrases.

2 Practise saying them.

**4a** Complete the conversation with the words in the box.

| Coffee | chicken | Nothing | sir | water |
|---|---|---|---|---|

| | |
|---|---|
| WAITER: | Yes, please? |
| CUSTOMER A: | Can I have a sandwich, please? A ¹_____ sandwich. |
| WAITER: | And for you, ²_____ ? |
| CUSTOMER B: | ³_____ for me, thank you. |
| WAITER: | And to drink? |
| CUSTOMER A: | Can I have ⁴_____ , please? |
| CUSTOMER B: | ⁵_____ for me, please. With milk. |
| WAITER: | Anything else? |
| CUSTOMER B: | No, thank you. |

**b** Work in groups of three. Practise saying the conversation.

**5** Work in groups of three. Prepare and practise a similar conversation. Change the information in the gaps with the words in the box or your own ideas.

| cheese | fish | madam | orange juice | pasta | tea |
|---|---|---|---|---|---|

Hi, Mum and Dad,

How are you?
Carolyn and I are here in Turkey. Our hotel is very comfortable. It's called Hotel Panorama. The people are very friendly, and the food and weather are fantastic.
We're on the beach now and we're very happy!

See you soon,
Jo

JAMES AND ANN HUMPHREYS
52 BOSTOCK ROAD
WOODLEY
OXFORDSHIRE
UNITED KINGDOM
OX52 3KD

# Writing
## Holiday messages

**1** Read the postcard and answer the questions.

1 Who is it from?
2 Who is she with?
3 Where are they?

**2** Read Carolyn's email to her friend. Complete the gaps with the words in the box.

| | | | |
|---|---|---|---|
| expensive | fantastic | friendly | on holiday |
| See you | We're | | |

**Carolyn**

**Subject:** Holiday in Turkey

Hi Sam,
I'm here [1]_____ in Turkey with Jo.
Our hotel is cheap but the people are very [2]_____ .The restaurants here are good, and the food isn't [3]_____ .
The weather here is [4]_____ . [5]_____ on the beach now!
[6]_____ soon,

Carolyn

**3** Write your own postcard or email. Include these things:

- a greeting
- a message (say where you are, who you're with, information about the food/weather/people, etc.)
- a message ending.

## AFTER UNITS 2 AND 3 YOU CAN ...

Ask and answer questions about people, jobs and nationalities.

Ask and answer questions about peoples' age.

Talk about your favourite food and drink.

Order food and drink in a café.

Write a short postcard or email.

# 04

# AROUND TOWN

## Vocabulary
### Places in a town

1   🎧 4.1 Look at the map. Listen, point to and repeat the places.

| | | | | |
|---|---|---|---|---|
| a café | a restaurant | a cinema | a hotel | a supermarket |
| a bank | a bus stop | a train station | a square | a park |
| a car park | a shopping centre | | | |

---

**PRONUNCIATION**

1 Listen again to the places in exercise 1 and mark the stress.
a cáfé   a rèstaurant

2 Practise saying them.

---

2   Write the places in exercise 1 in the correct place. Some words belong in more than one category.

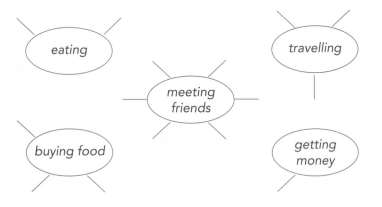

# Grammar focus 1
## Prepositions of place

**1** 🎧 4.2 Look at the pictures. Listen and repeat the prepositions.

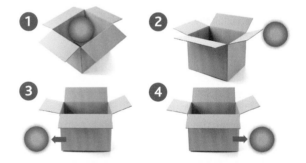

### GRAMMAR

**Prepositions of place**

| *in* | She is **in** the supermarket. The supermarket is in South Street. |
|---|---|
| *near* | The people are **near** the bus stop. |
| *on the left of* | The bank is **on the left of** the café. |
| *on the right of* | The restaurant is **on the right of** the cinema. |

**2** Look at the map. Are the sentences true (T) or false (F)?

1 The café is in the park.
2 The train station is near the cinema.
3 The bank is on the left of the supermarket.
4 The cinema is on the right of the restaurant.

**3a** Choose the correct answers.

1 The car park is near the *train station* / *bus stop*.
2 The supermarket is *on the left of* / *on the right of* the bank.
3 The café *is* / *isn't* in the square.
4 The bus stop is near the *hotel* / *café*.
5 The park *is* / *isn't* near the train station.
6 The supermarket is in *Victoria Street* / *Station Road*.
7 The hotel is *on the left of* / *on the right of* the car park.
8 The shopping centre is *on the left of* / *on the right of* the cinema.

**b** 🎧 4.3 Listen and check your answers.

### PRONUNCIATION

**1** Listen again to the sentences in exercise 3a.

**2** Practise saying them.

**4a** Write three true sentences and three false sentences about the map.

**b** Work in pairs. Say your sentences to your partner. Are they true or false?

> The bank is on the left of the hotel.

> False! It's on the left of the supermarket.

**Unit 4, Study & Practice 1, page 104**

## Grammar focus 2
### *there is* and *there are*

1 **Look at the picture. Are the sentences true (T) or false (F)?**

   1 There are three children in the picture.
   2 There are two men in the picture.
   3 There's a woman in the picture.
   4 There are two taxis in the picture.

**GRAMMAR**

*there is* and *there are* – positive

| Singular | **There's** a man in the picture. (= there is)<br>**There's** a taxi in the picture. (= there is) |
|---|---|
| Plural | **There are** two cafés in the picture. (NOT there're)<br>**There are** three women in the picture. |

2a **Complete the sentences with 's or *are*.**

   1 There _____ three apples on the table.
   2 There _____ a bottle of water in my bag.
   3 There _____ an Italian restaurant near here.
   4 There _____ two people in the car.
   5 There _____ a bank next to the supermarket.
   6 There _____ five children in the cinema.

b 🎧 4.4 **Listen and check your answers.**

**PRONUNCIATION**

1 🎧 4.5 **Listen to the pronunciation of *th-* in these words. Practise saying the words.**

   there  they  the  this  that  these  those

2 **Practise saying the sentences in exercise 2a.**

3a **Look again at the picture. Write four sentences.**

b **Work in pairs and compare your sentences.**

   *There are two yellow taxis.*

   *There's an Italian restaurant.*

Unit 4, Study & Practice 2, page 104

## Reading
### Places to visit in York

1 Jay is from the USA. Today he's in York, a city in England. Read the comments on the travel forum and find:

   • the name of the cathedral in York: *York Minster*
   • the name of a hotel in York: _____
   • the name of a restaurant in York: _____
   • the name of a town near York: _____

**Mar 11  1.45 p.m.**
**jaybee   PLACES TO VISIT IN YORK**
Hi! I'm in York for three days ... any ideas for places to visit?
**Mar 11**
**MariaM – Re: Places to visit in York**
York's a fantastic city. There's a famous cathedral – York Minster – it's 600 years old! And there's a big university, there are some beautiful old streets in the city centre ... and there are a lot of nice cafés and restaurants.
**Mar 13**
**jaybee – Re: Places to visit in York**
Thanks!! Is there a good hotel in York? Somewhere in the city centre, not expensive, please!!
**Mike – Re: Places to visit in York**
Yes. There's a hotel in Mount Street: its name is the King's Hotel. It's very friendly and it isn't expensive.
**jaybee – Re: Places to visit in York**
Thanks. Are there any good restaurants near the hotel?
**Mike – Re: Places to visit in York**
My favourite Indian restaurant in York is Akash. It's near the King's Hotel and the food is very good.
**Timbo – Re: Places to visit in York**
A nice town near York is Market Weighton. Go by bus or taxi – there isn't a train station. There aren't any big shops, but there are some fantastic cafés!

**2** Read the text again. Are the sentences true (T) or false (F)?

1 The cathedral is 600 years old.
2 The King's Hotel is very expensive.
3 Mike's favourite Indian restaurant is in the King's Hotel.
4 There's a train station in Market Weighton.
5 The shops in Market Weighton are very big.

# Grammar focus 3
**_there is_ and _there are_ – positive, negative and questions**

**1**  Read the text again. Underline all the examples of _there is_ and _there are_. Which are positive, which are negative and which are questions?

## GRAMMAR

_there is_ and _there are_ – positive, negative and questions

|   | Singular | Plural |
|---|----------|--------|
| + | **There's an** old university. (= there is) | **There are some** beautiful old streets. **There are a lot of** nice cafés. |
| – | **There isn't a** train station. (= there is not) | **There aren't any** big shops. (= there are not) |
| ? | **Is there a** good hotel in York? Yes, **there is.** / No, **there isn't.** | **Are there any** good restaurants near the hotel? Yes, **there are.** / No, **there aren't.** |

**2a**  Choose the correct answers.

1 There is **a / any** beautiful square in the city centre.
2 There are **any / some** taxis near the train station.
3 Is there **a lot of / a** cinema near here?
4 Are there **a / any** buses to the shopping centre?
5 There aren't **some / any** cheap hotels in the city centre.
6 There are **any / a lot of** big shops in this area.
7 There isn't **a / an** train station in my town.
8 Are there **a / any** supermarkets near here?

**b**  🎧 4.6 Listen and check.

**3a**  Write the name of a place in your country where:

1 there's a famous university.
2 there are some very good shops.
3 there aren't any people.
4 there's a famous square.
5 there are a lot of good restaurants.
6 there isn't a train station.

**b**  Work in pairs and take turns. Talk about the places in your country.

> In Italy, there are some very good shops in Milan, but they are very expensive.

Unit 4, Study & Practice 3, page 105

## Reading and vocabulary
### Natural features

1 🎧 4.7 Match the pictures with the words in the box. Listen and check.

a beach    a hill    an island    a lake    a mountain
a rainforest    a river    the sea

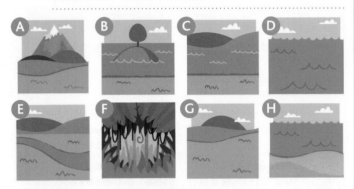

2 🎧 4.8 Choose the correct answers. Listen and check.

1 The Mediterranean is a famous *river / sea*.
2 There are about 1,400 *seas / islands* in Greece.
3 There are over three million *lakes / jungles* in Canada.
4 The Nile is a *river / sea*. It's about 6,650 km long.
5 There are about 40,000 different plants in the Amazon *hill / rainforest*.
6 Mount Fuji is a *rainforest / mountain* in Japan. It's 3,776 metres high.
7 Copacabana is a famous *beach / island* in Brazil.
8 There are seven *beaches / hills* in the city of Rome.

3 Read about Paris and answer the questions.

1 What is the name of the river in Paris?
2 How many islands are there in the river?
3 Are there any beaches in Paris?
4 Is Paris near the sea?
5 Are there any mountains in Paris?
6 Are there any hills?
7 Are there any forests in Paris?
8 Where are the lakes?

IT'S A FACT!
In Paris, there are approximately 400 parks, 7,000 cafés and 2.2 million people.

In Paris, there is a river called the Seine. In the river, there are two islands with buildings on them, called Île Saint-Louis and Île de la Cité. There aren't any beaches because Paris isn't near the sea. There aren't any mountains, but there are a lot of hills – Montmartre is 130 metres high. There aren't any forests in Paris, but there are lakes and forests near the city.

# Task

## Talk about your home town

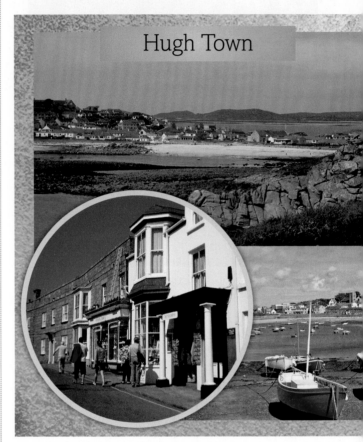

Hugh Town

## Preparation Listening

1 Work in pairs. Look at the photos of Hugh Town and Gotemba. What can you see? Which is a small town? Which is a big town?

2a Look at the places in the table below. Which do you think are in Hugh Town and which are in Gotemba?

| | Hugh Town | Gotemba |
|---|---|---|
| beaches | | |
| lakes | | |
| parks and hills | | |
| shops / shopping centre | | |
| cinemas | | |
| restaurants | | |

b 🎧 4.9 Listen and complete the table.

3 Listen again and tick the questions and answers you hear in the Useful language box.

Gotemba

**a Questions**
What famous places are there near your town?
What places are there in your town?
Is there a (cinema/hotel) in your town?
Are there any (beaches/lakes) near your house/town?

**b Answers**
There aren't any (famous places).
There are some fantastic (beaches/mountains).
No, there isn't a (park/hotel) in my town.
Yes, there are a lot of lakes near my town.
It's (beautiful/great)!
They're (fantastic/very nice)!

# Task Speaking

1 Prepare to talk about a town. Make some notes using the table in Preparation exercise 2a to help you. Look at the Useful language box to prepare your questions and answers. Ask your teacher for any words/phrases you need.

> Useful language a and b

2 Work in pairs and take turns. Ask and answer questions about your town.

> What famous places are near your town?

> There's a famous beach called Copacabana.

> And are there any mountains … ?

3 Work in different pairs. Talk about what's near your town.

## SHARE YOUR TASK

Practise talking about what's near your town.

Film/record yourself talking about what's near your town.

Share your film/recording with other students.

# LANGUAGE LIVE

That's Market Street.

## Speaking
### Asking for directions

**1** ▶ Watch conversations 1–3. How many people give directions?

**2** Watch again. Number the phrases in the order you hear them.

**Conversation 1**
a Yes. There's a bank in Market Street.
b Thank you.
c Excuse me.  *1*
d Yes?
e Is there a bank near here?

**Conversation 2**
a I don't know. Sorry.
b Where's Market Street?
c Excuse me?  *1*

**Conversation 3**
a No problem.
b Thank you.
c Market Street. It's down there ... on the right.
d You're welcome.
e Oh sorry!  *1*
f Where's Market Street?

**3** Watch conversation 4. Where's the bank? Tick the correct answer.

a In Market Street, on the left.
b In Market Street, on the right.
c He doesn't know.

**4a** Work in pairs. Complete the gaps to make a conversation.

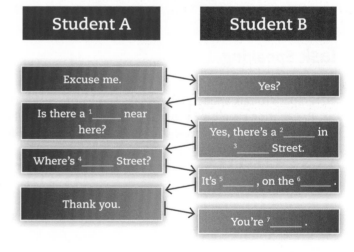

**Student A**

Excuse me.

Is there a ¹_____ near here?

Where's ⁴_____ Street?

Thank you.

**Student B**

Yes?

Yes, there's a ²_____ in ³_____ Street.

It's ⁵_____ , on the ⁶_____ .

You're ⁷_____ .

**b** Practise your conversation.

## MY TOWN

The name of my town is Cáceres. It's in Spain. Cáceres is famous for its historic town centre. There's a beautiful cathedral in Cáceres, and there are a lot of good restaurants and small shops in the centre. There's also a famous university in Cáceres. My favourite restaurant is El Horno. It's in the centre of Cáceres, in Calle San Martín. There's a National Park near Cáceres. Its name is Monfragüe. It's a beautiful place!

# Writing
## Your town

**1** Read about Vicky and answer the questions.

    **1** What nationality is Vicky?
    **2** Which town is she from?
    **3** What is her town famous for?
    **4** What's the name of her favourite restaurant? Where is it?
    **5** Where is the Monfragüe National Park?

**2** Complete the sentences about your town.

    **1** The name of my town is _____ .
    **2** It's in _____ .
    **3** It's famous for _____ .
    **4** There's a beautiful _____ and a _____ .
    **5** There are a lot of _____ .
    **6** My favourite _____ is _____ .
       It's in _____ .
    **7** Near my town, there's a beautiful _____ .

**3** Write a paragraph about another town you know or like. Use the questions below to help you.

- What is the name of your town?
- Where is it (country)?
- Why is it famous?
- Is there a cathedral/university, etc.?
- What shops and restaurants are there? What's your favourite? Where is it?
- What place can you visit near the town?

### AFTER UNIT 4 YOU CAN ...

Describe a picture and write simple sentences about it.

Ask and answer questions about your home town.

Ask for and give directions.

Write a short description of your home town.

# 05

# HOME AND FAMILY

## IN THIS UNIT

- Grammar: Possessive 's; Present simple (*I*, *you*, *we*, *they*); Present simple questions (*I*, *you*, *we*, *they*)
- Vocabulary: Family; Verbs with noun phrases
- Task: Present your personal profile

## Vocabulary
### Family

1a 🎧 5.1 Look at the photos and listen to the family words.

- brother and sister
- father and son
- mother and daughter
- parents and children
- husband and wife
- grandmother and grandson
- grandfather and granddaughter
- grandparents and grandchildren

b Work in pairs. Which of the family words in exercise 1a are:

- male?
- female?
- male or female?

---

### PRONUNCIATION

1 Listen again to the words in exercise 1a and mark the stress.

brother     sister

2 Practise saying them.

---

2a Underline the odd one out.

1 son, <u>parent</u>, daughter
2 husband, wife, child
3 grandparent, brother, sister
4 brother, son, wife
5 wife, children, mother
6 sister, father, husband

b Work in pairs and check your ideas.

**Possessive 's**

Dylan is Sonia's brother. (NOT Dylan is the brother of Sonia.)
Sonia and Laura are Dylan's sisters.
Tom's father's name is George.

**2a** Read the sentences in exercise 1 again. Rewrite the false sentences to make them true.

**b** 🎧 5.2 Listen to the correct sentences and check your answers.

**1** Listen again to the sentences in exercise 2b and notice the pronunciation of possessive 's.

**2** Practise saying the sentences.

**3** Write 's in the correct place in the sentences.

1 Jonny is Ali brother.
*Jonny is Ali's brother.*
2 My sister name is Suzanna.
3 Her brother name is Alex.
4 Tom is Kate husband.
5 My father name is Daniel.
6 Hugo and Harry are Sarah sons.
7 My teacher name is Amelia.
8 Kara is Maria daughter.

**4** Work in pairs. Tell your partner about four people in your family. Say his/her name and two more facts (e.g. age, job, country).

My brother's name is Jonas. He's twenty-five and he's a student.

My brother's name is Diego. He's seventeen and he's a student, too.

# Grammar focus 1
## Possessive 's

**1** Look at the family tree and read the sentences. Are the sentences true (T) or false (F)?

1 Dylan is Sonia's brother.
2 Tom is Helena's husband.
3 Sonia and Laura are Dylan's sisters.
4 Sonia's mother's name is Laura.
5 Alice is George's wife.
6 Helena is Tom's grandmother.
7 Tom's father's name is George.
8 Tony and Alice are Anna's grandparents.

| George | Helena | Tony | Alice |

| Tom | Anna |

| Dylan | Sonia | Laura |

Unit 5, Study & Practice 1, page 106

# Life in another country

**A** My name's Ellie. I'm from China, but I don't live there now – I study medicine at university in London. I live with two other students. They don't study medicine – they study engineering. We live in a flat near the university. Everything is expensive in London – so it's a small flat, but it's very nice!

**B** I'm David and this is my wife Sophie. We're from London, but now we live in Shanghai in China. We're very happy here! We don't work in an office. We work at Shanghai University – we teach English to university students. We have two children – our son Harry is 11 and our daughter Holly is nine. They go to the International School here in Shanghai. They study Chinese and they speak it really well now!

## Reading
### Life in another country

**1** Read about the people in the photos. Match the names in the box with the photos.

> David   Ellie   Harry   Holly   Sophie

**2** Are the sentences true (T) or false (F)?

1 Ellie is Chinese.
2 She's a teacher.
3 She is in London now.
4 David and Sophie are English.
5 They are happy in China.
6 They are students.
7 Their daughter is 11 years old.
8 Their children are at school in London.

## Grammar focus 2
### Present simple (*I, you, we, they*)

**1** Who says these sentences? Read the text again and write the names.

1 'I study in London.' _____
2 'My husband and I teach English.' _____
3 'We live with our parents.' _____
4 'My sister and I don't live in England now.' _____
5 'Our children don't go to university.' _____
6 'I don't have a big flat in London.' _____

**2a** Complete the sentences with the words and phrases in the box.

> don't go   don't have   don't live   live
> speak   study   teach   work

1 Ellie and her friends _____ in a flat.
2 David and Sophie _____ in London now.
3 David and Sophie _____ English to university students.
4 David and Sophie _____ at Shanghai University.
5 Harry and Holly _____ Chinese with their friends.
6 Harry and Holly _____ to school in England.
7 Ellie and her friends _____ at London University.
8 David and Sophie _____ three children.

b 🎧 5.3 Listen and check.

# Vocabulary
## Verbs with noun phrases

**1a** Write the phrases in the box next to the correct verb.

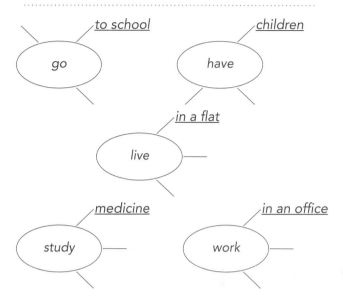

| a car | with your family | at university | languages |
|---|---|---|---|
| long hours | home for lunch | to work by bus | two brothers |
| in a house | for a big company | | |

*to school* — ( go )     *children* — ( have )

*in a flat* — ( live )

*medicine* — ( study )     *in an office* — ( work )

**b** 🎧 5.4 Listen and check.

> **PRONUNCIATION**
>
> **1** 🎧 5.5 Listen to ten sentences. Is each sentence positive (+) or negative (–)?
>
> **2** Listen again and repeat the sentences.

**3a** Write four sentences about you. Use the verb phrases in the box. Write two true sentences and two false sentences.

| I live in … | I don't live in … | I have … |
|---|---|---|
| I don't have any … | I study … | I don't study … |
| I work in/with/for … | I don't work in/with/for … | |

*I work in an office.*

**b** Work in pairs. Read your sentences to your partner. Can your partner guess which sentences are true and which are false?

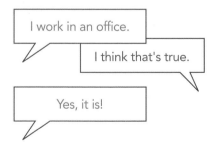

I work in an office.

I think that's true.

Yes, it is!

Unit 5, Study & Practice 2, page 106

IT'S A FACT!
Approximately one billion people in the world speak Chinese.

**2a** Read the sentences. Underline the verb phrases to make each sentence true for you.

1 I *don't live / live* in a flat.
2 I *don't have / have* a car.
3 I *don't study / study* Italian.
4 I *don't go / go* to work by bus.
5 I *don't work / work* for a big company.
6 I *don't study / study* at university.
7 I *don't live / live* with my family.
8 I *don't have / have* a sister.
9 I *don't go / go* home for lunch.
10 I *don't work / work* in an office.

**b** Work in pairs and compare your sentences.

**3a** Think of two people you know (e.g. your parents, two friends. Write five sentences about them using the verb phrases in exercise 1.

*Denise is my friend. She has three children and …*

**b** Work in pairs. Read your sentences to your partner.

## Grammar focus 3
### Present simple questions (*I, you, we, they*)

1 🎧 5.6 **Complete the questions with the verbs in the box. Listen and check.**

go   have   live   study   work

1 Where do you live?
2 Do you _____ in the town centre?
3 Do you live in a house or a flat?
4 Who do you live with?
5 Do you _____ any children?
6 Do you _____ or study near your home?
7 Do you _____ to work or school by car?
8 Do you _____ English at school?

2 🎧 5.7 **Listen to Mario answering questions 1–5. Underline his answers (a or b).**

1 a in a big city          4 a with my family
  b in a small town          b with my wife
2 a Yes, I do.             5 a Yes, I do.
  b No, I don't.             b No, I don't.
3 a in a house
  b in a flat

### GRAMMAR

| Present simple questions | Short answers |
|---|---|
| **Do** you **work** near home? | Yes, I **do**. (NOT Yes, I work.) |
| **Do** they **have** any children? | No, I **don't**. (NOT No, I don't |
| Where **do** you **live**? | work.) |

3 Write questions with *you* using the ideas in the box.

live alone                go to work or school at the weekend
work in an office         go to work or school by bus
have a car                work for a big company
study after work          have a big family

*Do you live alone?*

### PRONUNCIATION

1 🎧 5.8 **Listen to the questions. Notice that the pronunciation of *do* is weak.**
*Do you live alone?* /dəjuː/

2 **Practise saying the questions.**

4 Work in pairs and take turns. Choose eight questions from exercises 1 and 3. Ask and answer the questions.

Unit 5, Study & Practice 3, page 106

# Task
## Present your personal profile

### Preparation
#### Listening

1 🎧 5.9 **Listen to Talya talking. Tick the things she talks about.**

- her country
- her city
- her house/flat
- her job
- her favourite food
- her brothers/sisters
- her parents
- her grandparents

2a **Complete the table with information about Talya.**

| 1 age | 26 |
|---|---|
| 2 country | |
| 3 parents' home town | |
| 4 town/city you live in now | Istanbul |
| 5 people you live with | |
| 6 job | |
| 7 number of people in your family | |
| 8 jobs of people in your family | |

b Listen again and check.

3 Listen again and tick the phrases you hear in the Useful language box.

**a  Giving basic information about you**
My name is ... and I'm (26/33 ... ).
I'm from (Turkey/Japan ...).
I live in (Australia/the USA ... ) now.
My parents are from (a small town / the capital city ... ).

**b  Talking about your house/town/job**
I live (with my family/alone).
I live in (a flat/a house).
I'm (an artist/a student/an engineer ... ).
I study at university.
I work (for a magazine / in a school / in an office ... ).
I go to work by (bus/car).

**c  Talking about your family / important people**
My (brother's/sister's/father's/mother's) name is ...
He's/She's (a student).
They're (teachers).
They work for a big company.

## Task Speaking

1a  Make notes about your personal profile. Use the table in Preparation exercise 2a to help you. Ask your teacher for any words or phrases you need.

b  Divide your ideas into three parts and write a personal profile for you. Look at the Useful language box to help you.

> Useful language a–c

2  Work in groups and take turns. Present your personal profile.

# THINGS YOU DO

## IN THIS UNIT

- Grammar: Present simple (*he*, *she*, *it*); Present simple questions (*he*, *she*, *it*)
- Vocabulary: Activities – verbs; Likes and dislikes
- Task: Giving information about someone
- Language live: Making offers; Your classmate;

cook a meal

go to the gym

use a computer

listen to music

go out with friends

## Vocabulary
### Activities – verbs

**1a** 🎧 **6.1** Look at the pictures. Listen and repeat the verb phrases.

**b** Match the words and phrases in the box with the verbs below.

| | | | |
|---|---|---|---|
| dinner | computer games | to the cinema | your family |
| a laptop | magazines | a film | live music |

**watch:** TV, *a film*
1 **play:** tennis, _____
2 **read:** books, _____
3 **go out with:** friends, _____
4 **listen to:** music, _____
5 **go:** to the gym, _____
6 **cook:** a meal, _____
7 **use:** a computer, _____

**2** Work in pairs. Put the verb phrases from exercise 1 in the correct category.

- things you do at home
- things you do outside home
- things you do at home and outside home

watch TV

play tennis

read books

## Listening
### Two lives

**1a** Look at the photos of Tom and Annie. Which sentences do you think describe Tom and which describe Annie?

He/She:
1 cooks dinner for his/her family.
2 plays tennis every day.
3 doesn't go to the gym.
4 reads books a lot.
5 uses a computer a lot.
6 doesn't go out with friends a lot.

**b** 🎧 6.2 Listen to two people talking about Tom and Annie and check your ideas.

**2** Listen again. Are the sentences true (T) or false (F)?

1 Tom is 15 years old.
2 He is the winner of a cooking competition.
3 He reads books about food.
4 Annie is 60 years old.
5 She plays tennis with her sister.
6 She talks to her friends on a computer.

# Grammar focus 1
## Present simple (*he, she, it*)

**1** Look at the sentences in Listening exercise 1a. Which are positive and which are negative?

### GRAMMAR

Present simple (*he, she, it*)

| | |
|---|---|
| + | **He** cooks dinner for his family.<br>**My brother** watches TV every day.<br>The school **has** a new computer system. (NOT **It haves** or **It have**) |
| – | She **doesn't go** to the gym.<br>Her teacher **doesn't listen** to music.<br>My town **doesn't have** a cinema. |

### PRONUNCIATION

**1** 🎧 6.3 Listen to the verbs below and notice the pronunciation of *-s* and *-es* endings.

cooks  goes  has  listens  plays  reads  uses  watch**es**

**2** Practise saying the verbs.

**2** 🎧 6.4 Choose the correct answers. Listen and check.

1 My mother *cook / cooks* dinner every day.
2 He *play / plays* football with his friends.
3 Diana *don't use / doesn't use* the laptop every day.
4 My friends *go / goes* to the cinema a lot.
5 She *watch / watches* TV every day.
6 My parents *don't read / doesn't read* magazines.
7 Miguel *use / uses* a computer at work.
8 He *has / have* a lot of friends.

**3a** Write sentences about people you know. Use some of the ideas in the table and your own ideas.

*My friend Marcia reads magazines a lot.*

| My friend (Anita) | (don't) | listen(s) to | TV | every day |
|---|---|---|---|---|
| My brother/sister | (doesn't) | cook(s) | music | a lot |
| A lot of my friends | | use(s) | computer games | |
| My mother/father | | go(es) | football | |
| My grandparents | | go(es) out | dinner | |
| My son/daughter | | watch(es) | a laptop | |
| My husband/wife | | has/have | to the cinema<br>with friends | |

**b** Work in pairs. Tell your partner about people you know.

My father goes to the cinema a lot.

Really? My father watches TV a lot. He watches TV every day.

Unit 6, Study & Practice 1, page 108

# A good match?

## Reading
### A good match?

**1** Look at the photos. Read the information about six people and match each person with a photo.

**2** Read the information again and answer the questions.

How many people:
1 play tennis?
2 like going to the gym?
3 have a dog?
4 play computer games?

**3** Read the information again and complete the sentences.

   _Eddie_ travels a lot.
1 _____ plays the guitar.
2 _____ cooks a lot.
3 _____ listens to live music.
4 _____ doesn't like cooking.
5 _____ and _____ speak different languages.

**4** Work in pairs. Which of the people do you think are good friends?

> I think Hannah and Marco are good friends because she plays tennis and he plays tennis, too.

**Eddie** is 27. He's a businessman and he travels for his job. He likes learning different languages and eating the food in different countries. He reads magazines and likes playing computer games.

**Marina** is 31 and she's a doctor. She works a lot so she doesn't have much free time. She doesn't watch TV – she listens to music at home and she also listens to live music.

**Hannah** is 26 and she teaches young children in a school. She plays tennis at the weekend and she likes going out with her friends. She goes to restaurants a lot because she doesn't like cooking.

**Marco** is a teacher. He's 29 and he lives with two friends. He cooks for his friends and his favourite food is Japanese. He plays tennis a lot, but he doesn't like going to the gym.

**Sarah** is a student. She's 24 and she studies languages at university. She doesn't like going to the gym, but she likes walking in the park with her dog. She reads a lot of books – in different languages.

**Jack** is 28 and he's an accountant. He likes his job, but he has a lot of hobbies, too. He likes music and he plays the guitar. He goes out with his friends, listens to music and goes to the cinema.

# Grammar focus 2
## Present simple questions (*he, she, it*)

1  Match the questions with the answers in the box.

Yes, she does.   No, she doesn't.   Yes, he does.
No, he doesn't.   I don't know.

1 Does Jack play the guitar?
2 Does Marina listen to live music?
3 Does Marco like going to the gym?
4 Does Hannah like cooking?
5 Does Eddie play football?

### GRAMMAR

**Present simple questions (*he, she, it*)**

**Does** he **play** the guitar? (NOT Does he plays ...)
**Does** she **listen** to music?
**Does** she **like** cooking?

**Short answers**
Yes, he **does**. (NOT Yes, he plays.)
No, she **doesn't**. (NOT No, she doesn't like.)

2  Write questions using *he* or *she* and the words below.
1 have a pet
2 like Chinese food
3 watch TV a lot
4 go to the cinema
5 go out with his/her friends a lot
6 like cooking
7 go to the gym
8 travel a lot
9 play football

### PRONUNCIATION

1  🎧6.5 Listen to questions 1–4 in exercise 2. Notice the linking between *does he* and *does she*.

2  Practise saying the questions.

3a Work in pairs. Student A: Read the information about two women, Petra and Lola, on page 96. Student B: Read the information about two men, Stefan and David, on page 97.

b  Take turns to ask and answer the questions in exercise 2 to find out which man and woman make a good match.

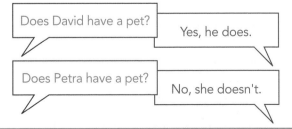
Does David have a pet? — Yes, he does.
Does Petra have a pet? — No, she doesn't.

Unit 6, Study & Practice 2, page 108

45

## Vocabulary
### Likes and dislikes

**1a** 🎧6.6 **Look at the pictures. Listen and repeat the words and phrases.**

| | | | |
|---|---|---|---|
| football | fast food | dogs | shopping |
| Chinese food | running | jazz | rock music |
| going to the cinema | horses | | |

**b** Work in pairs. Write the words and phrases from 1a in the correct place.

**Sports**: _football_, _____ , _____
**Food and cooking**: _____ , _____ , _____
**Music**: _____ , _____ , _____
**Free time activities**: _shopping_ , _____ , _____
**Animals and pets**: _____ , _____ , _____

**c** Add the words and phrases below.

| | | | | |
|---|---|---|---|---|
| basketball | cats | pop music | spicy food | walking |

**2** Look at the verb phrases in the sentences. Write them on the lines.

1 I **like** playing football.
2 I **love** shopping.
3 I **hate** fast food.
4 I **don't like** dogs.
5 I **don't mind** jazz – it's OK.

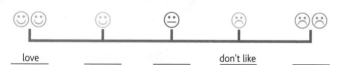

love _____ _____ don't like _____

**3** 🎧6.7 **Listen and complete the sentences.**

1 I _____ horses.
2 I _____ rock music.
3 I _____ playing basketball.
4 I _____ running.
5 I _____ Chinese food.

**4** Work in pairs. Talk about things you like/dislike using the ideas in exercise 1a.

> I hate football.

> Me too! But I love basketball.

# Task

## Giving information about someone

## Preparation Listening

**1a** Read the 'Find someone who ...' quiz. Match 1-10 with the correct category.

• food • music • sport • pets • free time

**b** Work in pairs. Write questions for each phrase in the quiz using *you*.

*Do you go to the cinema a lot?*
*Do you like spicy food?*

**2a** 🎧6.8 Listen to Daniel doing the quiz. Answer the questions below.

1 Which questions does he ask?
2 Who answers *yes* to his questions?

**b** Listen again and tick the questions and answers you hear in the Useful language box (parts a and b).

**3a** 🎧6.9 Listen to Daniel talking about the results of his quiz. Which sentences are true (T) and which are false (F)?

1 Stella goes to the cinema a lot.
2 Alex likes spicy food.
3 Juliet plays the guitar.
4 Stella has a cat.
5 Ali plays basketball.
6 Kim listens to live music a lot.

*IT'S A FACT!*
The top three sports in the world are football, cricket and hockey.

**b** Listen again and tick the phrases you hear in the Useful language box (part c).

# Find someone who ...

1  ... goes to the cinema a lot.
2  ... likes spicy food.
3  ... plays the guitar.
4  ... has a cat.
5  ... plays basketball.
6  ... listens to live music a lot.
7  ... cooks foreign food.
8  ... goes to the gym a lot.
9  ... reads books.
10 ... likes rock music.

## USEFUL LANGUAGE

**a Questions**
Do you go to (the cinema / the gym) a lot?
Do you like (spicy food / rock music)?
Do you play (the guitar / basketball)?
Do you have a (cat/dog)?

**b Answers**
No, I don't like (going to the cinema).
Yes, I do. I love (spicy food).
Yes, I do. I like (listening to live music) – especially (jazz).
No, I don't. I play the (piano) but I don't play the (guitar).
No, I don't – I hate (cats).

**c  Giving information about someone**
He/She goes to (the cinema / the gym) a lot.
He/She likes (spicy food / horses).
He/She loves (basketball / jazz / spicy food).
He/She doesn't play (the guitar / football).
He/She doesn't have a (cat/dog).
He/She hates (going to the gym / reading books).
His/Her favourite (sport/food/music) is (basketball / Chinese food).

## Task Speaking

1a  Read the questions in Preparation exercise 1b again. Write one more question. Ask your teacher for any words/phrases you need.

b  Ask different students in the class all of your questions. Use the Useful language box to help you.  Write the answers.

> Useful language a and b

2a  Prepare to tell the class about different students using the answers to your questions. Use *He/She* ... and the Useful language box (part c) to help you.

> Useful language c

b  Tell the class about different students.

> Maria cooks foreign food. She likes cooking Mexican food. Emre doesn't like reading books, but he loves reading magazines.

## SHARE YOUR TASK

**Practise giving information about different people.**

**Film/Record yourself giving information about different people.**

**Share your film/recording with other students.**

# LANGUAGE LIVE

## Writing
### Your classmate

**1** Read about Kara, Alan and Maria. Match the texts with the photos

**Kara** likes cooking and she likes cooking food from Asia. Her speciality is pilaff, a dish with rice, meat and vegetables.

**Alan** likes animals. His favourite animals are dogs and he has a pet dog called Lulu. He doesn't have a cat.

**Maria** likes music and she plays the piano. She doesn't listen to pop music, but she likes classical music. Her favourite composer is Bach.

**2a** Read the examples with *and* and *but*.

Alan likes animals **and** he has a pet dog called Lulu. Maria doesn't listen to pop music, **but** she likes classical music.

**b** Complete the sentences with *and* or *but*.

**1** Adam loves food, _____ he doesn't like cooking.
**2** Elly doesn't like dogs, _____ he likes cats.
**3** Sam likes rock music _____ he plays guitar in a group.
**4** My friend loves Italian food _____ her favourite dish is pasta.
**5** Michelle likes animals, _____ she doesn't have a pet.
**6** Luis loves classical music, _____ he doesn't play an instrument.

**3** Complete the sentences with the names of people you know.

**Food**
**1** _____ (name) likes _____ food and his/her favourite dish is _____ .
**2** _____ (name) loves cooking and her/his speciality is _____ .

**Animals**
**3** _____ (name) loves animals and he/she has a pet _____ called _____ .
**4** _____ (name) likes animals, but he/she doesn't have a pet.

**Music**
**5** _____ (name) doesn't like classical music but he/she likes _____ .
**6** _____ (name) likes _____ music and he/she plays the _____ .

**4** Write some similar sentences about a friend or member of your family.

# Speaking
## Making offers

**1** Match the pictures with the words and phrases in the box.

chocolates    popcorn    a bottle of water    tissues

**Would you like some popcorn?**

**2** ▶ Watch the video. Complete the sentences with *Jim*, *Alice* or *Jim and Alice*.

1 _____ doesn't/don't buy anything to eat.
2 _____ have/has water to drink.
3 _____ eat(s) chocolates.
4 _____ eat(s) popcorn.
5 _____ is/are very sad at the end of the film.
6 _____ use(s) a tissue.

**3a** Watch again and choose the correct answers.

1 JIM:    Would you like something to *eat / drink*?
2 ALICE:  *No, thanks. / Yes, please*.
3 JIM:    Are you *OK / sure?*
4 ALICE:  Yes, I'm *fine / OK,* thank you.
5 JIM:    How about something to *drink / eat*?
6 ALICE:  *Yes, please. / No, thanks*.
7 JIM:    Would you like *a chocolate / some popcorn*?
8 JIM:    *Here / There* you are.
9 JIM:    How about *a chocolate / some popcorn*?
10 ALICE: *Yes, please. / No, thank you*.

**b** Watch and listen to the key phrases and check your answers.

**4a** Work in pairs. Read and practise the conversation.

**A:** Would you like something to eat? How about a sandwich?
**B:** No, thanks.
**A:** Are you sure?
**B:** Yes, I'm OK, thanks.
**A:** How about something to drink?
**B:** Yes, please. A coffee, please.
**A:** OK. Two coffees.

**b** Prepare and practise a similar conversation.

## AFTER UNITS 5 AND 6 YOU CAN ...

Ask and answer questions about your family.

Ask and answer questions about your life.

Write and present your personal profile .

Ask and answer questions about people's likes and dislikes.

Ask for and give information about people .

Offer and accept/refuse things to eat and drink.

# 07

## YOUR TIME

## Vocabulary
### Daily routines and times

1a ∩∩7.1 Look at the pictures. Listen and repeat the verb phrases.

| In the morning | In the afternoon | In the evening |
| --- | --- | --- |
| get up | have lunch | have dinner |
| have breakfast | finish work | go to bed |
| go to work | get home | |
| start work | | |

b When do you usually do these things?

2a ∩∩7.2 Read the times in the box. Match them with the clocks. Listen and check.

| | | | |
| --- | --- | --- | --- |
| seven o'clock | one fifteen | nine thirty | twelve forty-five |
| eleven o'clock | six thirty | two forty-five | eight fifteen |

3 ∩∩7.3 Listen and write the times you hear.

*1 – 6 o'clock*

4 Work in pairs and take turns. Point to different clocks/times on this page and ask your partner *What's the time?*

> What's the time?
>
> It's eleven o'clock.

# Reading
## Routines around the world

**1** Read about John and Ruthie. Answer the questions about each person.

   **1** What is his/her job?
   **2** Does he/she like his/her job?

My name's John and I live in Johannesburg in South Africa. I'm a restaurant manager and I love my job. I don't have much free time because my restaurant is very busy. I always get up early – at about 6 in the morning – and I have breakfast. I usually have coffee and bread for breakfast. I go to work at 7 o'clock and I start work in the restaurant at 7.30. I have lunch – a big lunch in my restaurant – at 1 p.m.
I don't usually have dinner. I finish work at about 10:30 p.m. or sometimes 11 o'clock.

My name's Ruthie and I live in Buenos Aires in Argentina. I'm a singer and I always work in the evening. I get up late – about 11:30 a.m. – because I never work in the morning. I don't usually have breakfast, but I have lunch at about 12:30 p.m. I go to work at about 5 o'clock and I start work at 5:30. I usually finish work at 12 a.m., but it's sometimes 1.00 a.m. I get home at about 1:30 or 2 and go to bed. I love my job, but I sometimes feel very tired!

**2** Read the texts again and answer the questions.

   **1** What time does Ruthie get up?
   **2** Does she have breakfast?
   **3** What time does she start work?
   **4** What time does she get home?
   **5** What time does John get up?
   **6** Does he have breakfast?
   **7** Where does he have lunch?
   **8** What time does he finish work?

**3a** Choose five verb phrases from the box in Vocabulary exercise 1a and write sentences about you.

   *I get up at 6:30.*

   *I have lunch at home.*

**b** Work in pairs and compare your sentences.

# Grammar focus 1
## Frequency adverbs

**1a** Read the texts again. Underline all the frequency adverbs: *usually*, *sometimes*, *always* and *never*.

**b** Write *usually* and *don't usually* in the correct place.

| always | | sometimes | | never |
|---|---|---|---|---|
| 100% | _____ | | _____ | 0% |

---

### GRAMMAR

**Frequency adverbs**

**Notice the word order.**
I **always work** in the evening.
I **usually finish** work at 12 a.m.
I **sometimes feel** very tired.
I **don't usually have** dinner.
I **never work** in the morning.

NOT I **work always** in the evening.
NOT I don't **have usually** dinner.

---

**2** 🎧 7.4 Rewrite the sentences using the words in brackets. Listen and check.

   **1** I start work at 7 a.m. (never)
   **2** I feel tired in the morning. (usually)
   **3** I have breakfast. (not usually)
   **4** I go to work by train. (sometimes)
   **5** I have lunch in a restaurant. (always)
   **6** I go to bed late. (usually)
   **7** I work in the evening. (never)
   **8** I get up early. (not usually)

**3a** Change the sentences in exercise 2 to make them true for you.

**b** Work in pairs and compare your sentences.

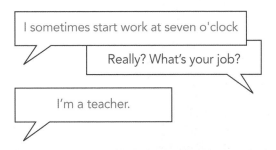

I sometimes start work at seven o'clock

Really? What's your job?

I'm a teacher.

▶ Unit 7, Study & Practice 1, page 110

# Vocabulary
## Days and times

**1** 🎧 **7.5 Read and listen to the days of the week.**

**Monday**          **Saturday**
**Tuesday**         **Sunday**
**Wednesday**
**Thursday**
**Friday**

**2** 🎧 **7.6 Listen and underline the day you hear.**

1 <u>Monday</u> / Sunday
2 Saturday / Sunday
3 Tuesday / Thursday
4 Wednesday / Saturday
5 Thursday / Friday
6 Tuesday / Thursday
7 Saturday / Thursday

**3a** Answer the questions with day(s) of the week.

1 Which day is your favourite?
2 Which day is your favourite TV programme on?
3 Which day is it today?

**b** Work in pairs and take turns. Ask and answer the questions in exercise 3a.

**4a** 🎧 **7.7 Listen to the conversations. Write the answers, including the day and time.**

When's your:
1 English class?   *On Monday at 7.30.*
2 doctor's appointment?
3 tennis lesson?
4 party?
5 football match?
6 favourite TV programme?
7 meeting?
8 exam?

**b** Work in pairs and take turns. Ask and answer the questions in exercise 4a. Say true or invented answers, including the day and time.

> When's your tennis lesson?
>
> On Saturday at one forty-five.

**IT'S A FACT!**
Tourism is the main industry in New Zealand with over 2 million visitors every year.

# Listening
## The Kawhia Kai Festival

**1a** Look at the photos and read the questions about the Kawhia Kai Festival in New Zealand. Can you guess any of the answers?

1 What does the festival celebrate?
  a food from New Zealand
  b food from the local area
2 When is the festival?
  a 6th February
  b 16th February
3 Why does it happen on that day?
  a because it's Independence Day in New Zealand
  b because it's Carnival in New Zealand
4 Where does the festival take place?
  a in the town and on the beach
  b in the streets and in people's houses
5 Who are the visitors?
  a local people only
  b local people and tourists
6 How many people are there?
  a about 1,000
  b about 10,000

**b** 🎧 **7.8 Listen and check.**

**2** Work in pairs and answer the questions.

1 What festivals are there in your country?
2 Which is your favourite?

# Grammar focus 2
## Present simple *Wh-* questions

**1** Match the question words in 1–6 with the meanings a–f. Use the questions in Listening exercise 1a to help you.

| | |
|---|---|
| **1** what | **a** a person |
| **2** who | **b** a number |
| **3** where | **c** a reason |
| **4** when | **d** a thing |
| **5** why | **e** a time |
| **6** how many | **f** a place |

**2** Complete the questions using *do*, *does*, *is* and *are*.

1 When _____ you have dinner?
2 Where _____ she work?
3 How many cars _____ there?
4 What _____ they like eating?
5 When _____ your birthday?
6 Who _____ he live with?
7 Why _____ you go by bus?
8 Where _____ the children?

### GRAMMAR

**Present simple *Wh-* questions**

**Notice the word order.**

What **does** the festival **celebrate**? (NOT What the festival **does celebrate**?)
Why **does** it **happen** on that day?
When **do** you **go**?
What **do** people **eat**?
When **is** the festival? (NOT When **does** the festival **be**?)
Who **are** the visitors?
How many people **are** there?

**3a** Choose the correct answers.

1 **A:** *What* / *Why* is your favourite special day or festival?
   **B:** It's the Cambridge Music Festival.
2 **A:** *Where* / *What* do people do?
   **B:** People listen to live music – singers and musicians.
3 **A:** *Who* / *When* is the festival?
   **B:** It's in the summer ... in July.
4 **A:** *Where* / *How many* does it take place?
   **B:** It's in a park in Cambridge.
5 **A:** *Who* / *How many* people are there?
   **B:** I think there are usually about 10,000 people.
6 **A:** *Who* / *Why* do you go with?
   **B:** I always go with six friends.
7 **A:** *Why* / *What* do you go?
   **B:** Because we all love music ... and it's a really fun festival.

b 🎧 **7.9 Listen and check your answers.**

### PRONUNCIATION

**1** 🎧 **7.10 Listen again to the questions in exercise 3a.** Notice the pronunciation of the question words.

**2** Practise saying them.

**4a** Think of a special day in your country or a country you know about. Prepare to answer the questions in exercise 3a.

b Work in pairs and take turns. Ask and answer questions to find out about your partner's special day.

> What is your favourite special day or festival?

> It's Carnival!

Unit 7, Study & Practice 2, page 110

## Vocabulary
### Prepositions with time expressions

**1a** Work in pairs. Number the words in order, from the beginning to the end of the day.

afternoon
midnight
midday
morning – 1
evening

**b** Work in pairs and take turns. Ask and answer the questions in the quiz.

### Are you a 'morning person' ... ?

1 When do you get up on weekdays?
2 When do you get up at the weekend?
3 What do you usually do on Sunday morning?
4 Do you have breakfast every day?
5 Do you like doing exercise in the morning?

**2a** Look at the time expressions in the box and write them next to the correct preposition.

| weekdays | the weekend | Sunday morning |
|---|---|---|
| the morning | the afternoon | three forty-five |
| day | weekend | |

**1 on**: Friday, _____ , _____
**2 in**: the evening, _____ , _____
**3 at**: two o'clock, _____ , _____
**4 every**: week, _____ , _____

**b** 7.11 Listen and check.

**3a** Choose the correct answers.

### ... or are you an 'evening person'?

1 When do you go to bed **on / at / in** weekdays?
2 When do you go to bed **on / at / in** the weekend?
3 What do you usually do **on / in / at** Saturday evening?
4 Do you cook dinner **on / in / every** day?
5 Do you like doing exercise **on / in / at** the evening?

**b** Work with a different partner. Ask and answer the questions in exercises 1b and 3a. Is your partner a 'morning person' or an 'evening person'?

# Task

## Give a mini-talk

## Preparation Listening

**1** Match the activities in the box with the photos. What time of day do people usually do these activities?

| going for a walk | having a coffee |
|---|---|
| running | doing T'ai Chi |
| going to a restaurant | reading a newspaper |

**2a** 7.12 Listen to Mei giving a mini-talk about morning routines in China. Number the things in the order you hear them.

- morning routine for young people
- morning routine for working people and older people
- what most people have for breakfast

**b** Listen again and decide if the statements are true (T) or false (F).

1 Most Chinese people get up at 7.30.
2 Most Chinese people drink tea for breakfast.
3 Young people start school with exercise.
4 Working people sometimes buy breakfast from a café.
5 Older people do exercise in the park after breakfast.

**3a** 7.13 Listen to Aleksi giving a mini-talk about food and meals in his country, Russia. Which of the things in the list does he NOT talk about?

breakfast    lunch    dinner    special meals

**b** Listen again to Mei and Aleksi and tick the phrases you hear in the Useful language box.

## USEFUL LANGUAGE

**a  Saying what people do**

In (Russia/China/Argentina), we usually (have/cook/eat) …

Most people (drink tea/eat/cook food at home) …

(Russian/Italian/Spanish) people usually (have/eat/drink) …

A typical (lunch/dinner) in (Russia/Poland/Japan) is …

**b  Time expressions**

Most people get up (early/late/at 6.00 …)

They sometimes (do exercise before breakfast).

The family (talks/watches TV) during (dinner/lunch).

After dinner, many (Russian/Chinese) people like (drinking tea / talking).

## Task Speaking

**1a**  Prepare to give a mini-talk about your country or a country you know about. Choose one of the topics in the list.

- Morning routines  • Evening routines  • Food and meals

**b**  Use Preparation exercises 2a or 3a to help you. Ask your teacher for any words/phrases you need and look at the Useful language box to help you.

>Useful language a and b

**2**  Work in groups and take turns. Give your mini-talk.

### SHARE YOUR TASK

**Practise giving your mini-talk.**

**Film/record yourself giving your mini-talk.**

**Share your film/recording with other students.**

# LANGUAGE LIVE

**Are you free on Saturday?**

## Speaking
### Making an arrangement

**1a** ▶ Watch the first part of the video. Where do Sally and Angie arrange to go on Saturday?

**b** Watch again and choose the correct answers.

1 They arrange to go to *a club / a concert / see a film*.
2 It's at *City Hall / the OK Club / the City Cinema*.
3 It's on *Thursday / Friday / Saturday*.
4 It starts at *7:30 / 8:00 / 8:30*.
5 They decide to meet at *City Hall / Sally's house / the City Cinema*.

**2** Watch the second part of the video. Choose the correct answers.

1 They arrange to go to *a club / a concert / see a film*.
2 It's at *City Hall / the OK Club / the City Cinema*.
3 It's on *Thursday / Friday / Saturday*.
4 It starts at *7:30 / 8:00 / 8:30*.
5 They decide to meet at *City Hall / Sally's house / the City Cinema*.

**3a** Watch the whole video and number the phrases in the order you hear them.

a Are you free this weekend?
b What time?
c It's on Saturday.
d See you there.
e How about a film?
f There's a concert at the City Hall.
g When is it?
h How about a night out?
I Yes. Good idea!

**b** ▶ Watch and listen to the key phrases and check your answers.

---

### PRONUNCIATION

1 ▶ Watch and listen again to the key phrases.

2 Practise saying them.

---

**4a** Work in pairs. Complete the telephone conversation with the words in the box.

| Saturday | cinema | this weekend | night out |
|----------|--------|--------------|-----------|
| 8 o'clock | film | | |

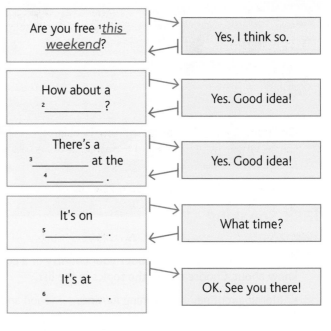

**Student A**          **Student B**

Are you free ¹*this weekend*? → Yes, I think so.

How about a ²_____? → Yes. Good idea!

There's a ³_____ at the ⁴_____. → Yes. Good idea!

It's on ⁵_____. → What time?

It's at ⁶_____. → OK. See you there!

**b** Practise your conversation. You can change the information in the gaps.

# Writing
## Making arrangements by text message and email

**1** Read the text messages below. Where do Jan and Steve arrange to go? When?

> Hi, Jan. How are you? Are you free on Saturday? Steve

> Hi, Steve! I think so. Why? Jan

> How about a film? *Rachel's Friends* is at the Park Cinema at 8.30.

> Good. I'd like to see that. Meet me at the Park Cinema at 8.15.

> OK. See you at 8.15!

**2** Work in pairs. Complete the text message conversation with your own ideas.

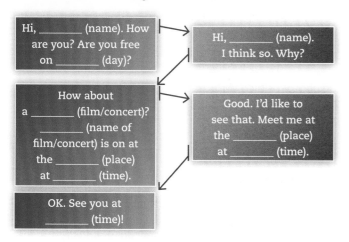

> Hi, _____ (name). How are you? Are you free on _____ (day)?

> Hi, _____ (name). I think so. Why?

> How about a _____ (film/concert)? _____ (name of film/concert) is on at the _____ (place) at _____ (time).

> Good. I'd like to see that. Meet me at the _____ (place) at _____ (time).

> OK. See you at _____ (time)!

**3** On Friday, Jan receives an email from her sister, Carrie, who lives in Paris. Read the email and answer the questions

   **1** What does Carrie want to do on Saturday?
   **2** Why is this a problem for Jan?

**Subject:** Surprise!

Hi Jan,
Surprise! Patrick and I are back in London for a few days ... and we have something very important to tell you! Are you free on Saturday? ... How about 8 o'clock? Where can we meet?
Carrie xxx
PS Don't say anything to Mum and Dad.

**4** EITHER write Jan's text message to Steve about Saturday night. Include these things.

- a greeting (*Hi ...* )
- say you can't come to the cinema on Saturday (*Sorry, but ...* )
- give a reason (*My sister ...* )
- suggest another day (*Are you free ...* )

**OR write Jan's email to Carrie about Saturday night. Include these things.**

- a greeting
- say you can meet her on Saturday night
- suggest a place/time (*How about ... ?*)
- a message ending (*See you ...* )

# YOU CAN DO IT!

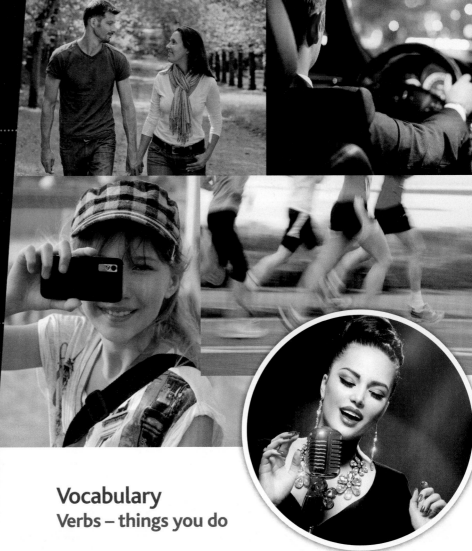

## Vocabulary
### Verbs – things you do

1 Look at the photos. Which verbs in the box can you see?

| | | | | |
|---|---|---|---|---|
| dance | drive a car | paint a picture | play chess | ride a bike |
| run | sing | swim | take photographs | walk |

2a Choose the correct answers.

1 I *take* / *play* a lot of photographs when I go on holiday.
2 I *swim* / *walk* to work every day because I don't like going by bus.
3 I love *swimming* / *driving* in the sea when I go on holiday.
4 I usually *play* / *paint* chess with my grandfather on Sunday afternoons.
5 I like *dancing* / *talking* when I go to a party with my friends.
6 I *sing* / *run* in the park at the weekend because I want to keep fit.
7 I always *walk* / *paint* a picture of the beach when I go on holiday.
8 I never *drive* / *ride* my car to the town centre because it's so busy.
9 I *run* / *ride* a bike to work in the summer but not in the winter.
10 I like listening to music in the car and *talking* / *singing* the songs.

b 🎧 8.1 Listen and check.

3a Which of the sentences in exercise 2a are true for you? Rewrite the false sentences to make them true for you.

b Work in pairs and compare your sentences.

> I take a lot of photographs when I go on holiday! Do you?

> No, I don't …

# Reading
## Amazing people!

**1** Read the text about amazing people. What abilities do they have?

## Amazing people!

*You Magazine* finds some amazing people who can do amazing things!

• Vadim Ivanov is from Russia and he's a chess player. He plays chess very well and he sometimes plays a lot of chess games at the same time. In fact, he can play over 300 chess games at the same time! He doesn't always win them all – but his record is playing 310 games and winning 282 of them!

• Alvaro and Alicia Sánchez are twins and they live in Argentina with their parents. They can't walk because they are only nine months old, but they can swim. In fact, they can swim 25 metres in the swimming pool. They go swimming every day and they love it!

• Emiko Kimura is 20 years old and she is an art student from Japan. She can't paint in the same way as her friends because she doesn't have any hands. She can paint with her feet and she wins a lot of competitions because her pictures are fantastic. Mostly, she likes painting pictures of people.

**2** Read the text again. Are these statements true (T) or false (F)?

  **1** Vadim Ivanov plays chess against over 300 people at the same time.
  **2** He always wins all the games.
  **3** Alvaro and Alicia Sánchez are babies.
  **4** They walk to the swimming pool every day.
  **5** Emiko studies art in Japan.
  **6** She is very good at painting.

**3** Discuss with other students. Do you know anyone who has similar abilities to the people in the text?

# Grammar focus 1
*can/can't*

**1** Complete the sentences with the verb phrases.

| | | |
|---|---|---|
| can swim | can play | can paint |
| can't paint | can't walk | can't win |

  **1** Vadim Ivanov _____ chess very well.
  **2** He _____ every game.
  **3** Alvaro and Alicia Sánchez _____ .
  **4** They _____ because they are babies.
  **5** Emiko Kimura _____ with her hands.
  **6** She _____ with her feet.

### GRAMMAR

*can/can't*

| I/You/He/She/ We/They | **can** play chess. |
|---|---|
| | **can** swim very well. |
| | **can't** run very fast. (= cannot) |
| | **can't** ride a bike. (= cannot) |

**2** 🎧 8.2 Write sentences using the prompts and *can* (✓) or *can't* (✗). Listen and check.

He / **play** tennis / ✓
*He can play tennis.*

  **1** He / **play** chess / ✗
  **2** They / **swim** 25 metres / ✓
  **3** She / **remember** all her friends' birthdays / ✗
  **4** He / **play** the piano / ✗
  **5** He / **cook** well / ✓
  **6** They / **drive** / ✗
  **7** You / **speak** a foreign language / ✓
  **8** I / **run** fast / ✗
  **9** She / **read** music / ✓
  **10** They / **dance** very well / ✗

### PRONUNCIATION

**1** Listen to the sentences again. Notice the pronunciation of *can* and *can't*.

/kæn/  /kɑːnt/

**2** Practise saying the sentences.

**3a** Think about you, your friends and people in your family. Rewrite the sentences in exercise 2.

*My cousin Dimitri can play chess.*

*I can't swim 25 metres.*

  **b** Work in pairs and compare your sentences.

Unit 8, Study & Practice 1, page 112

# Grammar focus 2
## Questions with *can*

**1** Match the photos with the job adverts below.

> ### DO YOU WANT TO BE A DANCE TEACHER?
> Can you sing, dance or play the piano?
> email: info@danceteachersdirect.com

> ### Do you want to be a personal trainer?
> Can you swim, run and play tennis?
> If yes … this is the job for you!
> **Call Mick on 07789 566433.**

> ### Do you want to be a nanny?
> Nanny for friendly family with three children.
> Can you drive a car, cook well and speak English?
> Phone 0845 677879 and speak to Annie.

**2a** 🎧 **8.3** Olivia wants a job for the summer holidays. Read the job adverts and listen. Tick the things Olivia can do and cross the things she can't do.

**b** Which job do you think is good for Olivia? Why?

---

### GRAMMAR

**Questions with *can***

| Questions | Short answers |
|---|---|
| **Can** you **dance**? | Yes, I/you/he/she/we/they **can**. |
| **Can** he/she **play** tennis? | No, I/you/he/she/we/they **can't**. |
| **Can** they **speak** English? | |

---

**3a** Write questions using *can* and the prompts.

you / sing well  *Can you sing well?*
**1** you / play tennis
**2** you / swim
**3** you / run fast
**4** you / cook well
**5** you / play the guitar
**6** you / ride a bike
**7** you / drive a car
**8** you / speak three languages

**b** 🎧 **8.4** Listen to conversations with the questions in exercise 3a. Does each person answer *yes* or *no*?

---

### PRONUNCIATION

**1** Listen again to the conversations in exercise 3b. Notice the pronunciation of *can* in the questions and the short answers.

**2** Practise saying the questions.

---

**4a** Work in pairs. Ask and answer the questions in exercise 3a. Find three things your partner can do but you can't do.

**b** Tell the class.

> Maria can play tennis, but I can't. She can swim, but I can't …

Unit 8, Study & Practice 2, page 112

## Reading and vocabulary
### Parts of the body

1 🎧 8.5 Listen to the parts of the body in the box. Which of these can you see in the photos?

| | | | |
|---|---|---|---|
| arm(s) | ear(s) | eye(s) | finger(s) |
| foot (feet) | hand(s) | head | leg(s) |
| mouth | nose | thumb(s) | toe(s) |

**PRONUNCIATION**

1 Listen again to the parts of the body in exercise 1.

2 Practise saying the words.

2 Work in pairs and look at the pictures. Ask and answer questions with your partner.

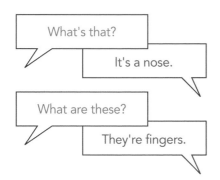

What's that?

It's a nose.

What are these?

They're fingers.

IT'S A FACT!
Your eyes are the same size all your life, but your ears don't stop growing.

3a Complete the text with the words in the box.

| | | | | | | |
|---|---|---|---|---|---|---|
| eyes | feet | hands | hand | head | nose | thumb |

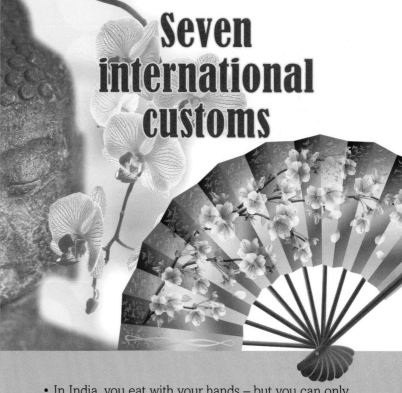

# Seven international customs

- In India, you eat with your hands – but you can only use your right ¹_____ .
- In Thailand, you can't put your ²_____ on a chair – it isn't polite.
- In Japan, you can't blow your ³_____ in public – it isn't polite.
- In Dubai, you shake ⁴_____ when you meet someone – but you can only use your right hand.
- In the USA, when you talk to someone, you can show interest by looking at his or her ⁵_____ .
- In Britain, you can say 'OK' or 'I like it' by holding your ⁶_____ up.
- In Bulgaria, you can say 'yes' by moving your head from side to side, and you can say 'no' by moving your ⁷_____ up and down.

b 🎧 8.6 Listen and check your answers.

4a Read the text again. Tick the things that are the same in your country and cross the things that are different.

b Work in pairs and compare your ideas.

In my country, it's the same as in Japan … you can't blow your nose in public.

Really? It's OK in my country.

## Grammar focus 3
### Review of questions

**1** Complete the questions below with the words in the box.

active   exercise   run   team   toes   watching

1 How fast can you _____?
2 Are you interested in _____ sport on TV?
3 How _____ are you?
4 When do you usually do _____?
5 Can you touch your _____?
6 Do you like playing _____ games; for example, basketball?

**2a** 🎧 8.7 Listen to two people asking and answering the questions in exercise 1. Number the questions in the order you hear them.

**b** Listen again and match the answers with the questions in exercise 1.

1 Yes, I love it.
2 No, I hate them.
3 No, I can't.
4 Not very fast.
5 I'm not very active.
6 I sometimes run for the bus.

---

### GRAMMAR

**Review of questions**

1 Notice the word order of questions with *be*.
   **Are you** interested in watching sport on TV?
   How active **are you**?
2 Notice the word order of questions with *can*.
   **Can you** touch your toes?
   How fast **can you** run?
3 Notice the word order of questions with other verbs.
   **Do** you **like** playing team games?
   When **do** you do exercise?

---

**3** 🎧 8.8 Write the words in the correct order to make questions. Listen and check.

1 like doing / you / do / What sports?
2 ten kilometres / you / Can / run?
3 you / Do / every day / walk / to school or work?
4 you / on your hands / stand / Can?
5 days a week / do / How many / you / do / exercise?
6 usually / you / up the stairs / Do / run?

**4** Work in pairs. Ask and answer eight of the questions from exercises 1 and 3.

Unit 8, Study & Practice 3, page 113

---

# Task

## Do a class survey

### Preparation Listening and reading

**1** Look at the survey. Match the photos with the four categories.

**2** 🎧 8.9 Listen to Bindi doing the first part of the survey with a friend. Answer the questions.

1 How many questions does Bindi's friend ask?
2 Is Bindi good with numbers?

**3a** Listen again and tick the questions you hear in the Useful language box (part a).

**b** Listen again and tick the answers you hear in the Useful language box (part b).

### Task Speaking

**1a** Read the questions in the survey again and make a note of your answers. Ask your teacher for any words/phrases you need and look at the Useful language box (part b) to help you.

> Useful language b

**b** Ask and answer the questions with other students. Write notes about their answers.

> Useful language a and b

**2** Work in pairs. Look at your notes and report the results of the survey for you and other students in the class.

I'm good with words. I like languages and I'm good at spelling.

That's interesting! Manuel is also good with words. He can speak four languages!

# What are your skills and interests?

## 1  Are you good with numbers?

1 Do you like maths?
2 Can you do this in your head: 356 + 567?
3 How good are you at remembering phone numbers?

## 2  Are you musical?

1 Can you play a musical instrument?
2 What kind of music do you listen to?
3 Are you good at singing?

## 3  Are you artistic?

1 Can you paint a picture of a person?
2 Are you interested in going to art galleries?
3 Do you like taking interesting photographs?

## 4  Are you good with words?

1 How many languages can you speak?
2 Are you good at spelling?
3 Do you like writing essays?

## SHARE YOUR TASK

**Practise talking about your skills and interests.**

**Film/record yourself talking about your skills and interests.**

**Share your film/recording with other students.**

My name's Alice. I'm 22 years old and I'm from Basel in Switzerland.
I'm good at languages. I can speak German, French, English and I want to study Italian, too!
I'm interested in music and I can play the piano and the guitar.
I'm not a sporty person but I can play chess and I can ski very well.

My name's Ozbek and I'm 31 years old. I'm from Ankara in Turkey.
I'm good at languages. I can speak Turkish, German and English. I want to study in the United States.
I can't play a musical instrument but I like music. My favourite singer is the American singer Kelly Clarkson.

## Writing
## Describe your skills and interests

**1** Read the texts and answer the questions.

1 Where is Alice from?
2 Can she speak French?
3 What musical instruments can she play?
4 Is she a sporty person?
5 How old is Ozbek?
6 How many languages can he speak?
7 Can he play a musical instrument?
8 Who is his favourite singer?

**2** Read the information about capital letters.

• We use capital letters at the beginning of a sentence and with names.
*My name's Alice.*
• We also use capital letters for cities/countries/languages/nationalities.
*Basel   London   New York*
*Switzerland   Peru   Australia*
*German   French   Italian*

**3** Read the text about Mônica. Write capital letters in the correct places.

my name's mônica and i'm from são paulo in brazil. i'm 28 years old. i'm good at languages. i can speak portuguese, spanish, italian and english. i love learning languages. i can't play a musical instrument but i like listening to music, especially brazilian music. my favourite singer is marisa monte. she's from brazil.

**4** Make some notes about you. Use these ideas to help you.

• your name
• your age
• where you're from (town/city and country)
• good at / not good at languages
• languages you can speak
• languages / other things you want to study
• interested in music?
• play musical instruments?
• sports/games you can play

**5** Write a paragraph about your skills and interests. Use the text about Alice and your notes to help you.

Can I sit here?

# Speaking
## Making requests

**1** ▶ Watch the video and choose the correct answers.

1 Ross is a *university student* / *teacher*.
2 Ross is *at the cinema* / *in a lecture hall*.
3 Ross is *early* / *late*.
4 Ross *has* / *hasn't* got a pen.
5 Ross *takes notes* / *sleeps* during the lecture.

**2** Watch again. Who says the phrases below?
Write R (Ross) or A (Another person).

1 Can I sit there?
2 Yes, of course.
3 Can you move your bag, please?
4 Can I have a pen, please?
5 Sorry, I don't have one.
6 Here you are.
7 Can you be quiet, please?
8 Can I see your notes?
9 No, you can't.

**3a** Choose the correct answers.

1 **A:** Excuse me. Can you take a photo of me and my friend?
   **B:** *Sorry, I don't have one.* / *Yes, of course.*
2 **A:** Can I have a bottle of water, please?
   **B:** *Here you are. That's one euro, please.* / *No, thanks*.
3 **A:** Can you clean the board for me, Luis?
   **B:** *Yes, of course.* / *Yes, here you are.*
4 **A:** Can you spell your name, please?
   **B:** *Yes, it's D-A-V-I-D.* / *My name's David.*
5 **A:** Can I see your dictionary, please?
   **B:** *Yes, here you are.* / *Yes, it is.*
6 **A:** Excuse me. Can you tell me the time, please?
   **B:** *It's Friday.* / *It's 8 o'clock.*

**b** Work in pairs. Practise saying the conversations.

**AFTER UNIT 8 YOU CAN ...**

Talk about your own and other people's abilities.

Ask and answer questions about people's abilities

Describe your skills and interests

Make and respond to requests

# 09

# NOW AND THEN

## IN THIS UNIT

- Grammar: Past simple of *be*: *was/were*; Questions with *was/were*
- Vocabulary: Months of the year; Ordinal numbers and dates; Years
- Task: Talk about your childhood

## Vocabulary
### Months of the year

1  🎧 9.1 Listen and number the months in the correct order.

| | | |
|---|---|---|
| **November** | **March** | **August** |
| **January** *1* | **May** | **June** |
| **October** | **February** | **December** |
| **September** | **July** | **April** |

---

### PRONUNCIATION

1  Listen again to the months. Mark the stress on each month.

Jánuary          Fébruary

2  Practise saying the months.

---

2  Work in pairs and answer the questions.

1  Which month is it now?
2  Which month is your birthday?
3  Which month is your favourite?
4  Which months are summer in your country?
5  Which months are winter?
6  When do people usually go on holiday in your country?

# Vocabulary
## Ordinal numbers and dates

1 🎧 9.2 **Listen and repeat the ordinal numbers.**

| | | | | | |
|---|---|---|---|---|---|
| **1st** | first | **5th** | fifth | **9th** | ninth |
| **2nd** | second | **6th** | sixth | **10th** | tenth |
| **3rd** | third | **7th** | seventh | **11th** | eleventh |
| **4th** | fourth | **8th** | eighth | **12th** | twelfth |

2a **Match the words in the box with the numbers.**

| | | | |
|---|---|---|---|
| twentieth | seventeenth | thirteenth | thirtieth |
| twenty-second | nineteenth | fifteenth | thirty-first |

| | | | |
|---|---|---|---|
| **a** 13th | **b** 15th | **c** 17th | **d** 19th |
| **e** 20th | **f** 22nd | **g** 30th | **h** 31st |

b 🎧 9.3 **Listen and check your answers.**

3 **Work in pairs and practise saying the ordinal numbers 1st to 31st.**

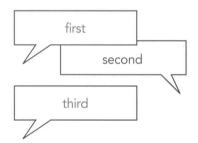

> first
>> second
> third

4 **Look at the dates. Write the missing words.**

| | | |
|---|---|---|
| **1st** March | = | the _____ of March |
| **2nd** May | = | the _____ of May |
| **3rd** February | = | the _____ of February |
| **4th** October | = | the _____ of October |
| **5th** November | = | the _____ of November |
| **9th** June | = | the _____ of June |
| **12th** April | = | the _____ of April |
| **20th** January | = | the _____ of January |

---

### PRONUNCIATION

1 🎧 9.4 **Listen to the dates in exercise 4 and notice the pronunciation.**

2 **Practise saying the dates.**

---

# Listening
## Special days

1 🎧 9.5 **Listen and match the dates with the special days.**

1 Canada Day
2 United Nations Day
3 St Patrick's Day in Ireland
4 Independence Day in Mexico
5 Freedom Day in South Africa

a 16th September
b 27th April
c 17th March
d 1st July
e 24th October

2a **Read the information about national holidays in Canada. How many does the text mention?**

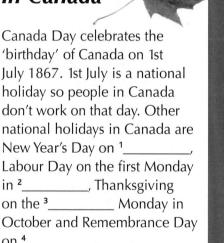

### National holidays in Canada

Canada Day celebrates the 'birthday' of Canada on 1st July 1867. 1st July is a national holiday so people in Canada don't work on that day. Other national holidays in Canada are New Year's Day on ¹_____, Labour Day on the first Monday in ²_____, Thanksgiving on the ³_____ Monday in October and Remembrance Day on ⁴_____ .

b 🎧 9.6 **Listen and complete the information.**

3a **Write down five dates, including:**

- national holidays or special days in your country.
- your birthday.
- the birthdays of people in your family.

b **Work in pairs. Tell your partner why these days are important.**

> My birthday is on the twenty-second of October.
>> Oh! My birthday is in October, too … it's on the sixth of October.

# In 1986 ...

**A** Ronald Reagan was President of the USA. He was ¹_____ years old.

**B** The number one film of the year was *Top Gun*, with American film star ²_____ . Other popular films in that year were *Crocodile Dundee*, with Australian actor Paul Hogan, and *Karate Kid*, with Italian–American actor Ralph Macchio.

**C** Germany wasn't a single country. There were ³_____ countries called 'Germany' – East and West. Bonn was the capital of West Germany and ⁴_____ was the capital of East Germany.

**D** The FIFA World Cup was in Mexico – and the winners were ⁵_____ . Diego Maradona was the captain of the winning team.

**E** There weren't any DVDs, laptops or iPads. Vinyl ⁶_____ were still popular.

**F** There were twelve countries in the European Union. ⁷_____ and Hungary weren't members of the European Union.

## Reading
### in 1986 ...

**1a** Read about the year 1986. Try to complete the text with the numbers and names in the box.

| | | | |
|---|---|---|---|
| two | 75 | Argentina | East Berlin |
| records | Poland | Tom Cruise | |

**b** 🎧 9.7 Listen and check your answers.

**2** Work in pairs and read the questions. How many can you answer?

1 Who is the President of the USA now?
2 What other films does Tom Cruise star in?
3 What is the capital of Germany?
4 Where is the next FIFA World Cup?
5 How many countries are in the European Union now?

## Grammar focus 1
### Past simple of *be*: *was/were*

**1** Look again at the text in Reading exercise 1a. Underline all the examples of *was, wasn't, were* and *weren't*.

**2** Complete the sentences about the 1950s with *was(n't)* or *were(n't)*.

1 Elvis Presley and Chuck Berry _____ big pop stars in the 1950s.
2 The Beatles _____ famous in the 1950s. Their first hit record _____ in 1963.
3 There _____ any colour televisions. All TV programmes _____ in black and white.
4 There _____ about 100 million cars in the world. Now there are about ten times more.
5 In the 1950s, there _____ three winners of the FIFA World Cup: Uruguay (1950), West Germany (1954) and Brazil (1958).
6 There _____ two Summer Olympic Games. They _____ in Finland and Australia.
7 There _____ any female presidents in the 1950s. One of the first female presidents in the world _____ Isabel Martínez de Perón in Argentina, from 1974 to 1976.

> **Unit 9, Study & Practice 1, page 114**

# Grammar focus 2
## Questions with *was/were*

**1** Read about Gemma Arterton. What is her nationality? Why is she famous?

### Gemma Arterton (born 1986)
Gemma Arterton is an English actor. Her parents were British and she was born in Gravesend in England in February 1986. Gemma and her sister Hannah were very happy as children. They were interested in acting. Gemma was a big fan of Disney films and her favourite character was Mickey Mouse. In the 2000s, she was a student at RADA (the Royal Academy of Dramatic Art) in London. After leaving RADA, she was in various films and TV roles. In 2008, she was in *Tess*, a classic drama series on British TV, and in 2010, she was in two films: *Clash of the Titans* and *Persia: The Sands of Time.*

**2** Match questions 1–6 with answers a–f.

1 Where was she born?
2 Was she happy as a child?
3 Were Gemma and her sister interested in acting?
4 Was her favourite Disney character Minnie Mouse?
5 When was she a student at RADA?
6 Was she in a film in 2008?

a Yes, she was.
b No, she wasn't.
c Yes, they were.
d No, it wasn't – it was Mickey Mouse.
e In the 2000s.
f In Gravesend in England.

## GRAMMAR

**Questions with *was* and *were***

***Yes/No* questions**
**Was** she happy as a child?
**Was** she in a film in 2008?
**Were** her parents British?
**Were** you a student in 2000?

**Short answers**
Yes, I/he/she **was**.
No, I/he/she **wasn't**. (= was not)
Yes, you/we/they **were**.
No, you/we/they **weren't**. (= were not)

***Wh-* questions**
When **was** she a student?
Where **were** her parents from?

IT'S A FACT!
The year 1986 was the United Nations International Year of Peace.

### Cary Grant (1904–86)

Cary Grant was a British–American actor, who died in 1986. His parents were British and he was born in Bristol in England in 1904. His real name wasn't Cary Grant – it was Archibald Leach. He was very unhappy as a child because his mother was ill. His first job was in the USA when he was 16. His first film was *Blonde Venus* with Marlene Dietrich in 1932. After that, he was famous for his roles in many films, including *Bringing up Baby* (1938) and *North by Northwest* (1959), and his last film was *Walk, Don't Run* in 1966. He was married five times – his last wife was Barbara Harris.

**3a** Look at the photo of Cary Grant. Complete the questions with *was or were*.

1 _____ Cary Grant's parents American?
2 _____ he born in the USA?
3 _____ his real name Cary Grant?
4 _____ he happy as a child?
5 Where _____ his first job?
6 _____ his first film *Walk, Don't Run*?
7 What _____ the names of four of his films?
8 What _____ the name of his last wife?

**b** Read the text and answer the questions in exercise 3a.

**4** Work in pairs and take turns. Think about the 1980s. Ask and answer the questions.

1 Were you born before, during or after the 1980s?
2 Do you know which actors were popular? What films were they in?
3 Which singers were popular? Do you like them?

> Were you born before, during or after the 1980s?
>> I was born before the 1980s. What about you?

> **Unit 9, Study & Practice 2, page 114**

## Vocabulary
### Years

**1a** 🎧 9.9 **Listen and say these years.**

| | | | | |
|---|---|---|---|---|
| 1986 | 1950 | 1999 | 1900 | 1914 |
| 2000 | 2009 | 2002 | 2012 | 2013 |

**b** 🎧 9.10 **Listen and write the years you hear.**

**2a** **When and where were these people born? Match the photos with the years and places in the box.**

| | |
|---|---|
| Mvezo, South Africa, 1918 | Chester, UK, 1968 |
| Barranquilla, Colombia, 1977 | Jamshedpur, India, 1982 |
| Manacor, Spain, 1986 | Los Angeles, USA, 2011 |

Rafael Nadal

Daniel Craig

Harper Beckham

Priyanka Chopra

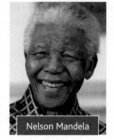
Nelson Mandela

Shakira

**b** 🎧 9.11 **Listen and check your answers.**

**c** **Work in pairs. Ask and answer questions about the people in exercise 2a.**

> When was Nelson Mandela born?
>
> He was born in …

**3** **Work with other students. Ask when and where each person was born.**

> When were you born?
>
> I was born in 1990.

> Where were you born?
>
> I was born in Kraków in Poland.

# Task

## Talk about your childhood

## Preparation Listening

**1a** 🎧 9.12 **Listen to Jack talking to his friend Marta about his childhood. Tick (✓) the things Jack talks about.**

- his family
- his best friend
- his pets
- his school
- his interests
- his favourite thing
- his house and town

**b** **Listen again and tick the questions and answers you hear in the Useful language box.**

**2** **What were Jack's answers? Listen again and check.**

**3** **Look again at the questions in the Useful language box. Match the questions with the categories.**

- People
- School and interests
- You

USEFUL LANGUAGE

a  Questions
Were you (tall/short)?
Were you (quiet or noisy / clean or dirty)?
Were you naughty at home?
Who was your (best friend / favourite person) in your family?
Were your (teachers / brothers and sisters) nice to you?
Were you nice to your (friends/brother/parents)?
What was your favourite subject?
Were you good at (sport/maths/music)?
Were you interested in (reading/sport)?

b  Answers
That's a difficult question.
I can't remember.
It was a long time ago!
I was(n't) good at (sport/music).
My favourite (subject/person/sport) was …
It was (great/fun/terrible)!

## Task Speaking

1a  Prepare to talk about your childhood. Look again at the questions in the Useful language box and think about your answers. Ask your teacher for any words/phrases you need and use the Useful language box to help you.

> Useful language a and b

b  Work in pairs. Choose six questions to ask your partner about his/her childhood. Take turns to ask and answer the questions.

2  Work with other students and take turns. Tell each other about your childhood.

> When I was a child, my favourite subject at school was music. I was good at playing the piano and …

SHARE YOUR TASK

Practise talking about your childhood.

Film/record yourself talking about your childhood.

Share your film/recording with other students.

71

# 10

# FAMOUS LIVES

Toni Morrison, writer

Henri Matisse, artist

Darcey Bussell, dancer

## IN THIS UNIT

- Grammar: Past simple – regular verbs; Past simple – irregular verbs
- Vocabulary: Verbs – life events; Creative jobs
- Task: Do a quiz
- Language live: Apologies and thanks

## Grammar focus 1
### Past simple: regular verbs (positive)

1a Match sentences 1–8 with the people in the pictures.

1 He died in France in 1954.
2 In 1988, she received a prize for her book, *Beloved*.
3 As a child she liked reading books.
4 She worked as the principal dancer at the Royal Ballet in London.
5 In 2009, she started work on a TV dance show.
6 In 1998 he created the search engine company Google.
7 He studied computer science at university.
8 He married Amélie Noellie Parayre in 1898.

b 🎧 10.1 Listen and check your answers.

> **GRAMMAR**
>
> Past simple: regular verbs (positive)
>
> 1 **For most verbs, add *-d* or *-ed*.**
>   He die**d** in France.
>   She receive**d** a prize for her book.
>   She like**d** reading books.
>   She work**ed** as the principal dancer.
>   She start**ed** work on a TV dance show.
>   He creat**ed** the company Google.
> 2 **For verbs ending in *-y*, add *-ied*.**
>   He stud**ied** computer science.
>   He marr**ied** in 1898.
> 3 **Notice that *I/you/he/she/it/we/they* use the same past verb forms.**

Larry Page, computer scientist

## Grammar focus 2
### Past simple: regular verbs (negative)

1   🎧 10.3 **Read about Leonardo da Vinci. Can you guess which three facts in the text are *not* true? Listen and check your ideas.**

Leonardo da Vinci was an artist, a scientist and a designer. He was born in the small town of Vinci in Italy in 1452. As a child, he studied painting in the city of Florence. In 1482, when he was 30, he moved to New York. He lived and worked there for many years.
Da Vinci was famous as a great artist. He painted *The Last Supper* in 1458 and *La Gioconda* (the *Mona Lisa*) in 1503. He was also a great designer. He designed early planes and bridges. In 1516, near the end of his life, he moved to France. He died in Italy in 1519, aged 67.

---

### GRAMMAR

**Past simple: regular verbs (negative)**

1 *did* + *not* + verb
   He **didn't move** to New York. (= did not)
   He **didn't paint** *The Last Supper* in 1458. (= did not)

2 Notice that *I/you/he/she/it/we/they* are all the same.
   I **didn't** study Chinese at school. (= did not)
   They **didn't** receive a prize. (= did not)

---

### PRONUNCIATION

1   🎧 10.2 **Listen to the Past simple forms below. Notice the pronunciation of the -*ed* endings. Complete the table.**

| died | liked | started | received |
|------|-------|---------|----------|
| studied | created | married | worked |

| /d/ | /t/ | /ɪd/ |
|-----|-----|------|
| *died* | *liked* | |

2   **Practise saying the Past simple forms.**

2   **Look at audio script 10.2 on page 000 and underline all the Past simple regular verbs.**

3   **Complete the sentences with the Past simple form of the verbs in brackets.**

   1 Larry Page _____ (love) computers as a child.
   2 He _____ (live) in Michigan, USA when he was young.
   3 Henri Matisse _____ (study) law in Paris before starting to paint.
   4 He _____ (die) at the age of 84.
   5 Toni Morrison _____ (move) to New York in 1964.
   6 She _____ (work) at Stanford University in the 2000s.
   7 Darcey Bussell _____ (marry) an Australian businessman in 1997.
   8 She _____ (receive) prizes for dancing in 1995 and 2006.

2   **Correct the information about Leonardo da Vinci, using the information in brackets.**

He studied painting in Paris. (Florence)
*He didn't study painting in Paris. He studied in Florence.*

   1 He moved to London in 1482. (Milan)
   2 He lived in Rome for many years. (Milan)
   3 He painted the *Mona Lisa* in 1458. (1503)
   4 He studied history. (maths)
   5 He designed cars. (planes)
   6 He liked drawing vegetables. (people)
   7 He moved to France in 1519. (1516)
   8 He died in Italy. (France)

3a   **Choose two of the people in the photos and write three false sentences about them.**

*Darcey Bussell lived in the USA.*

4a   **Work in pairs. How many facts can you remember about each person in the photos?**

b   **Say sentences about them.**

> Darcey Bussell lived in Australia when she was a child.
>> Yes ... and she married an Australian businessman.

b   **Work in pairs. Say your false sentences to your partner. Correct your partner's 'sentences.**

> Darcey Bussell lived in the USA.
>> No. She didn't live in the USA. She lived in Australia.

**Unit 10, Study & Practice 1, page 116**

**Unit 10, Study & Practice 2, page 116**

## Vocabulary
### Verbs – life events

**1** Look at the verb phrases and match them with pictures A–J.

1 leave (primary/secondary) school
2 go to university
3 leave university
4 pass your driving test
5 get your first job
6 start a business
7 meet your partner / someone special
8 get married
9 buy a house or flat
10 have children

**2a** Choose the correct verbs.

When do most people:

1 *get* / *have* married?
2 *buy* / *start* a house or flat?
3 *meet* / *have* children?
4 *go* / *leave* secondary school?
5 *pass* / *go* to university?
6 *leave* / *get* university?
7 *go* / *get* their first job?
8 *pass* / *have* their driving test?

**b** Work in pairs. Ask and answer the questions about your country or a country you know.

> In your country, when do most people pass their driving test?
>> When they're about 18 or 19, I think.

# Vivienne Westwood
## *queen of fashion*

Vivienne Westwood is a fashion designer. She was born in 1941 in the north of England. When she was 17, her family moved to London. She went to art school but she didn't become an artist … she became a teacher and got a job at a primary school. At the same time, she made jewellery and sold it in a market.

In 1961, Vivienne met Derek Westwood and they got married. They had a son, Ben, in 1963, but Vivienne and Derek didn't stay together. She met Malcolm McLaren, a businessperson and music manager, and they had a son, Joseph, in 1967.

Vivienne left her job as a teacher in 1971 and started a business with Malcolm McLaren. She designed clothes in the punk era of the 1970s and sold them in their first shop in London. She continued to design clothes and she bought other shops in the UK, Milan, Paris and Los Angeles.

For thirty years, she lived in a small flat, but in 2000, she bought a big house in London with her new husband, fashion designer Andreas Kronthaler. In 1990 and 1991, she won a prize, British Designer of the Year, and in 2005, she had a big show to celebrate her long career as a fashion designer.

**IT'S A FACT!**
The top four fashion capitals in the world are London, Milan, New York and Paris.

## Reading
### Vivienne Westwood

**1a** Work in pairs. Look at the pictures of Vivienne Westwood. Where do you think she is from? What do you think her job is?

**b** Read the text and answer the questions in exercise 1a.

**2** Read the text again. Are the statements true (T) or false (F)?

1 Vivienne Westwood was born in London.
2 She was an artist before she was a teacher.
3 She was a teacher in a primary school.
4 She had two sons.
5 She started designing clothes in the 1970s.
6 Her first shop was in Los Angeles.
7 She lives in a small flat in London.
8 She was British Designer of the Year in 2005.

**3** Work in pairs and answer the questions.

1 Do you like Vivienne Westwood's fashion style?
2 What other fashion designers do you know?
3 Are you interested in fashion?

*She went to art school but she didn't become an artist …*

# Grammar focus 3
## Past simple: irregular verbs (positive and negative)

**1a** Match the verbs with the Past simple irregular forms.

| | | | |
|---|---|---|---|
| 1 | become | a | went |
| 2 | buy | b | became |
| 3 | get | c | got |
| 4 | go | d | made |
| 5 | have | e | sold |
| 6 | leave | f | met |
| 7 | make | g | had |
| 8 | meet | h | left |
| 9 | sell | i | bought |
| 10 | win | j | won |

**b** 🎧 10.4 **Listen and check.**

**c** Read the text in Reading exercise 1b again and underline all the Past simple irregular verb forms.

## GRAMMAR

Past simple: irregular verbs

| + | She **went** to art school.
They **got** married.
She **bought** a big house. |
|---|---|
| − | She **didn't go** to art school. (= did not)
They **didn't get** married. (= did not)
She **didn't buy** a big house. (= did not) |

Notice that *I/you/he/she/it/we/they* are all the same.

## PRONUNCIATION

**1** 🎧 10.5 **Listen to the sentences in the Grammar box and notice the pronunciation of the Past simple forms.**

**2** Practise saying the sentences.

**2a** Complete the sentences using the Past simple form of the verbs in brackets.

1 I _____ (leave) my job in 2010.
2 She _____ (go) to university to study business.
3 He _____ (sell) his business for a lot of money.
4 They _____ (buy) a flat in the town centre.
5 I _____ (meet) my husband last year.
6 He _____ (win) a prize for his music.
7 They _____ (get) married on a beach.
8 She _____ (become) an actor in 1999.
9 They _____ (have) three children – two sons and a daughter.
10 He _____ (make) a lot of money from his business.

**b** 🎧 10.6 **Listen and check.**

**3a** Rewrite the sentences in exercise 2a using the negative form of the verbs in brackets.

**b** 🎧 10.7 **Listen and check.**

**4a** Draw two circles. In one circle, write six sentences about your life using the Past simple. In the other, write the years you did each event, in a different order from your sentences.

**b** Work in pairs. Show your sentences and years to each other. Try to match your partner's sentences with the correct years.

> I think you became a doctor in … 2004.

> No, I didn't become a doctor in 2004!

Unit 10, Study & Practice 3, page 117

## Vocabulary
### Creative jobs

**1** Look at the jobs in the box and answer the questions.

| | | | |
|---|---|---|---|
| architect | artist | dancer | film director |
| inventor | musician | singer | writer |

For which jobs do you need to be:

1 active?
2 good at painting?
3 good at maths?
4 good at science?
5 good with words?
6 good with people?
7 good with money?
8 good at making things?
9 good at playing a musical instrument?

---

### PRONUNCIATION

**1** 🎧 **10.8** Listen to the jobs in exercise 1. Mark the main stress on each job.

•architect  •artist

**2** Practise saying the jobs.

---

**2** Complete the sentences with the correct jobs from exercise 1.

1 Charles Dickens was a _____ . His books were often about people in London in the 1800s.
2 Frida Kahlo was a Mexican _____ . She painted many pictures of herself.
3 François Truffaut was a _____ . One of his most famous films was *The Last Metro*.
4 Sergei Rachmaninov was a Russian _____ . He played the piano.
5 Billie Holiday was an American _____ . One of her famous songs is *Lady Sings the Blues*.
6 Anna Pavlova was a _____ . She studied at the Imperial Ballet School in Russia.
7 Alexander Graham Bell was an _____ . He created the first telephone in 1876.
8 Ieoh Ming Pei was a Chinese _____ . He designed the Louvre Pyramid in Paris.

**3** Work in pairs and answer the questions.

1 Can you think of any more famous people for each job in exercise 1?
2 Do any of your friends or family have creative jobs?
3 Which of the jobs are you interested in?

> Do any of your friends do any of these jobs?
>> Yes, my friend Adriana is an architect.

# Task

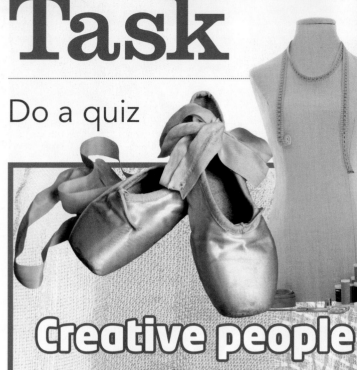

## Do a quiz

## Creative people

**1 George Lucas is a film director. He made:**
a the *Harry Potter* films.
b the *Lord of the Rings* films.
c the *Star Wars* films.

**2 Victoria Beckham is a fashion designer. Before that, she was:**
a a singer.
b a dancer.
c an artist.

**3 Gabriel García Márquez is a writer. In 1967, he wrote one of his most famous books:**
a *War and Peace.*
b *To Kill a Mockingbird.*
c *One Hundred Years of Solitude.*

**4 Rudolf Nureyev was a dancer. He died in:**
a New York.
b Moscow.
c Paris.

## Preparation Listening

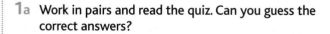

**1a** Work in pairs and read the quiz. Can you guess the correct answers?

**b** 🎧 **10.9** Listen to two people doing part of the quiz. How many questions do they talk about? Do they have the same answers as you?

**2** Listen again and number the phrases in the Useful language box in the order you hear them.

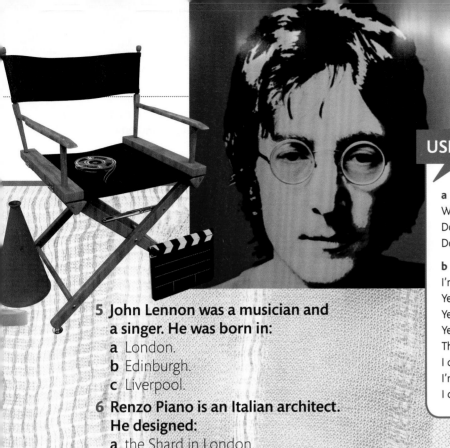

USEFUL LANGUAGE

**a Asking someone's opinion**
What do you think?
Do you know this one?
Do you have any ideas for this one?

**b Giving opinions**
I'm not sure, but I think …
Yes, I think so, too.
Yes, I think you're right.
Yes, I know this one.
That's right.
I don't know.
I'm not sure either.
I don't think it was …

**5 John Lennon was a musician and a singer. He was born in:**
a London.
b Edinburgh.
c Liverpool.

**6 Renzo Piano is an Italian architect. He designed:**
a the Shard in London.
b Burj Khalifa in Dubai.
c Madrid–Barajas Airport in Madrid.

**7 Gianni Versace was a fashion designer from Italy. He was born in:**
a 1926.
b 1946.
c 1966.

**8 J. K. Rowling is an English writer. She wrote:**
a the *Harry Potter* books.
b *Great Expectations*.
c *Murder on the Orient Express*.

## Task Speaking

**1a** Work in pairs and do the quiz. Ask your teacher for any words/phrases you need. Look at the Useful language box to help you.

>Useful language a and b

**b** How many of the answers did you know? Read the information on page 97 to check.

**2** Choose two of the people from the quiz and practise talking about them.

> Gianni Versace was an Italian fashion designer. He was born in …

SHARE YOUR TASK

Practise talking about the two people.

Film/record yourself talking about the two people.

Share your film/recording with other students.

# LANGUAGE LIVE

Thank you

## Writing
### Apologies and thanks

**1**  Read the text messages and emails. Which are apologies? Which are thanks?

**1**  Messages                               9:00AM

> Thanks for the lovely flowers. They are beautiful!
> Love Mum x

**2**  Subject:  Meeting

Sorry for the delay … here is the information about the business meeting on Friday. Hope this is OK. Please phone or email if you have any questions.

Regards
Jim P.

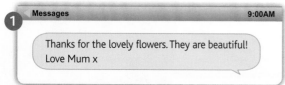

**3**  Messages                               1:40PM

> Thanks for the card. I was at the hospital for a few hours but I'm at home now and I'm OK. Visit me soon!  Vicky

**4**  Subject:  Invitation

Sorry I didn't answer your message. I didn't have internet access yesterday … so I didn't see your invitation!
Saturday is fine. See you then.
Mike

**2**  Read the answers below and match them with the text messages and emails in exercise 1.

**a**
Good to hear the accident wasn't serious. Sorry, I can't come to see you today. How about tomorrow about 5?

**b**
Thanks for this. I have one question: What time do we start on Friday? Do we have lunch before or after the meeting?

**c**
That's OK. I'm really pleased you can come. See you on Saturday. About 6?

**d**
You're welcome! Happy Mother's Day!

**3a**  Complete the sentences with *Thanks* or *Sorry*. Look at the messages in exercises 1 and 2 to check.

1  _____ for the lovely flowers.
2  _____ for the delay.
3  _____  for the card.
4  _____ I didn't  answer your message.
5  _____, I can't come to see you today.
6  _____ for this.

**b**  Look at the answers in exercise 2. Underline one way of answering when someone says *Thank you* and one way of answering when someone says *Sorry*.

**4a**  Choose two of the situations below. Write a text or email. Use the texts and emails in exercises 1 and 2 to help you.

1  Your friend sent you some flowers for your birthday. Write a text to thank him/her.
2  Send your colleague an email giving information about a meeting next week. Ask if he/she has any questions.
3  You are ill and at home. Write a text to thank your friend for his/her card and ask him/her to visit you.
4  Send your friend an email. Apologise for not answering before and say why. Accept his/her invitation.

**b**  Work in pairs. Read your partner's texts/emails and write a reply. Use the replies in exercise 2 to help you.

# Speaking
## Apologies and thanks

**1a** Work in pairs and discuss. Richard has an important business presentation. Which of these things are important?

- to arrive on time
- to wear smart clothes
- to buy a cup of coffee
- to bring his laptop
- to check the presentation on his laptop

**b** ▶ Watch the video. Which of the things in 1a did Richard do? Which things didn't he do?

**2a** Choose the correct answers.
1 Richard was **late** / **on time** for the presentation.
2 Richard came by **bus** / **train**.
3 Richard nearly drank the **man's** / **woman's** cup of coffee.
4 Richard **had some** / **didn't have any** problems with his laptop.
5 The man and woman **asked him some** / **didn't ask him any** questions.
6 The man and woman thought the presentation **was** / **wasn't** very good.

**b** Watch again and check your answers.

**3** Read the phrases below. Write A (apology), T (thanks) or R (response) next to each one.

I'm sorry I'm late.   *A*
1 Don't worry.
2 I'm sorry.
3 So sorry.
4 That's all right.
5 Thank you very much.
6 That's very kind.
7 You're welcome.
8 Thank you for the presentation.
9 No problem.

**4a** Complete the conversations with the words and phrases in the box.

### Conversation 1

| all right | bus | come |
| sorry | worry | |

**A:** Hello. I'm ¹_____ I'm late.
**B:** That's ²_____ .
**A:** The ³_____ didn't ⁴_____ .
**B:** Don't ⁵_____ . Sit down.

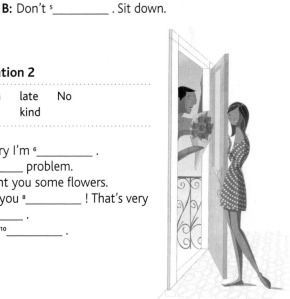

### Conversation 2

| very much | late | No |
| welcome | kind | |

**C:** Hi. Sorry I'm ⁶_____ .
**D:** ⁷_____ problem.
**C:** I bought you some flowers.
**D:** Thank you ⁸_____ ! That's very ⁹_____ .
**C:** You're ¹⁰_____ .

**b** Work in pairs and practise the conversations.

# 11

# TRAVEL

- Grammar: Past simple *Yes/No* questions; Past simple *Wh-* questions
- Vocabulary: Transport and travel; Time phrases; Holiday activities
- Task: Interview your partner about a holiday
- Language live: A blog about a journey: Travelling by train

## Vocabulary
### Transport and travel

1  🎧 11.1 Look at the pictures. Listen and repeat the words.

bike   boat   taxi   bus   car   plane   ship   train

2a  Read the sentences and decide if one or both words are possible answers.

1  **I usually go by** *bus / ship* **to work or school.**
2  I like reading when I **go on a** *bus / train* **journey**.
3  I usually **buy a single ticket** for a *car / bus* journey.
4  You can **buy a return ticket** for a journey by *bike / train*.
5  You can **buy a travel card** for *ships / buses* in my town.
6  In my town, *buses / trains* **are** usually **on time**.
7  When I go by *car / plane*, I **am** sometimes **early** for work.
8  When a *train / boat* **is late**, I read a book to pass the time.

b  🎧 11.2 Look at the verb phrases in **bold** and listen to the sentences.

3a  Read the sentences in exercise 2a again. Which ones are true for you or your town?

b  Work in pairs and compare your ideas.

# Transatlantic travel-the facts

Before the 1800s, people travelled across the Atlantic Ocean in boats – sailing boats. The journeys often took many weeks and they were very dangerous. In the 19th century, large ships began to cross the Atlantic. The journeys weren't so dangerous and they usually took several days, not weeks. An American ship called United States made a world-record journey in 1952 – crossing the Atlantic in three days, ten hours and 40 minutes.

In 1919, a British plane became the first plane to cross the Atlantic without stopping. The journey took about 72 hours. In 1927, the first passenger plane went across the ocean and in the 1930s, Germany started flying planes across the Atlantic with 60 passengers at a time.

Now, about 600 planes travel across the Atlantic every day and the average flight time from London to New York is six hours and 30 minutes. There are plans for a tunnel so people can travel by train under the Atlantic. They are only plans now – but who knows about the future?

## Reading
### Transatlantic travel-the facts

1 Read the text. Underline all the different types of transport.

2 Read the text again and decide if the sentences are true (T) or false (F).

1 In the 1700s, the journey across the Atlantic took about a week.
2 The world record for transatlantic travel by ship is about 3.5 days.
3 The first plane to cross the Atlantic was American.
4 The first plane took about three days to cross the Atlantic.
5 In the 1930s, American planes started to take passengers.
6 About 600 planes now travel across the Atlantic every week.

3 Work in pairs and discuss. What is your favourite way of travelling?

## Grammar focus 1
### Past simple *Yes/No* questions

1 Choose the correct answers.

1 Did the first transatlantic plane journey take about three days?
*Yes, it did. / Yes, it was.*
2 Did people fly across the Atlantic in the 1930s?
*Yes, they did. / Yes, they were.*
3 Was the first transatlantic plane American?
*No, it didn't. / No, it wasn't.*
4 Were the first transatlantic journeys easy?
*Yes, it did. / No, they weren't.*

### GRAMMAR

**Past simple *Yes/No* questions**

**Questions with be**
**Was** the first transatlantic plane American? *Yes, it was.*
**Was** the first transatlantic plane English? *No, it wasn't.*
**Were** the journeys by boat dangerous? *Yes, they were.*
**Were** the journeys by boat easy? *No, they weren't.*

**Questions with other verbs**
**Did** the journey **take** about three days? *Yes, it did.*
**Did** the journey **take** six weeks? *No, it didn't.*
**Did** people **travel** by plane in the 1930s? *Yes, they did.*
**Did** people **travel** by plane in the 1850s? *No, they didn't.*

2a Make questions about your journey to work/school this morning. Use the prompts in brackets.

1 _____ (you / buy) a single ticket?
2 _____ (you / have) a good journey?
3 _____ (you / be) tired?
4 _____ (you / buy) a travel card?
5 _____ (you / be) on time?

b 🎧 11.3 Listen and check.

### PRONUNCIATION

1 Listen again to the questions in 2b. Notice the linking between these words.
Did you ... ?     Were you ... ?

2 Practise saying the questions.

3 Work in pairs and take turns. Think about your journey to work/school this morning. Ask and answer questions about the journey. Use the questions in exercise 2a to help you.

*Did you buy a single ticket?*
*No, I didn't.*

Unit 11, Study & Practice 1, page 118

## Grammar focus 2
### Past simple *Wh-* questions

**1a** Match questions a–h with answers 1–8 in Listening exercise 2b.

  **a** Why did you go?
  **b** When did you go?
  **c** Where did you go?
  **d** Who did you go with?
  **e** How did you feel during the ride?
  **f** How much money did you raise?
  **g** How long were you there for?
  **h** What was the weather like?

**b** 🎧 11.5 Listen and check.

> **GRAMMAR**
>
> **Past simple *Wh-* questions**
>
> **Questions with *be***
>   What **was** the weather like?
>   How long **were** you there for?
> **Questions with other verbs**
>   Why **did** you **go**?
>   When **did** you **go**?
>   Where **did** you **go**?
>   Who **did** you **go** with?
>   How **did** you **feel** during the ride?
>   How much money **did** you **raise**?

**2** Complete the questions using the prompts in brackets.

  **1 A:** When _____ (she / leave) Australia?
    **B:** She left in December.
  **2 A:** Why _____ (you / go) to the town centre?
    **B:** I went for a job interview.
  **3 A:** How long _____ (you / be) there?
    **B:** We were there for a week.
  **4 A:** How _____ (they / feel) after the journey?
    **B:** They felt very tired.
  **5 A:** Where _____ (he / go) on holiday last year?
    **B:** He went to Argentina.
  **6 A:** Who _____ (you / visit) in London?
    **B:** I visited my sister.
  **7 A:** What _____ (the weather / be) like?
    **B:** The weather was terrible.
  **8 A:** How much money _____ (you / have)?
    **B:** We had £100.

**3a** Work in pairs. Student A: Read the information on page 96. Student B: Read the information on page 97. Take turns to ask the questions in exercise 1a. Make notes of your partner's answers.

**b** Work in pairs and discuss. Which of the three bike rides would you prefer to do? Why?

> Unit 11, Study & Practice 2, page 118

## Listening
### An amazing bike ride

**IT'S A FACT!**
The temperature in Death Valley, USA often gets up to 45°C in August.

**1** Work in pairs and look at the photo. Where do you think it is?

**2a** 🎧 11.4 Listen to an interview with Juliet and tick the things she talks about.

  • a bike ride
  • a sports camp
  • a charity
  • an organised group
  • a river
  • high mountains

**b** Listen again and choose the correct answers.

  **1** I went to the *USA / UK*.
  **2** I went in *June / July* last year.
  **3** I was there for about *two / three* weeks in total.
  **4** It was for *business / charity*.
  **5** I went with a group of *22 / 32* people.
  **6** It was very, very *hot / cold*.
  **7** I often felt really *hungry / tired*!
  **8** I raised about *£3,000 / £30,000*.

**3** Work in pairs and answer the questions.

  **1** When was the last time you went on a bike ride?
  **2** Where did you go?

# Vocabulary
## Time phrases

1 Read the text and underline seven more time phrases.

I first went to Greece <u>ten years ago</u>. I had a great time so I went back there in 2009. Last year, I went back again with my friend Michaela. We had a fantastic holiday. First, we went by plane to the capital city, Athens. Then, we went by boat to a beautiful island called Santorini. We stayed there for four days. After that, we visited three more islands. We had a great time, the weather was amazing and we didn't want to go home. But in the end, we got the boat back to Athens and went home.

2 Choose the correct answers.

1 I went to Argentina five years *last* / *ago*.
2 After *then* / *that*, we went to the airport.
3 In the *end* / *ago*, we got home at three o'clock in the morning.
4 I went on a train journey in Europe *on* / *in* 2012.
5 I went on a bike ride *last* / *after* month.
6 *Then* / *First*, we went to the beach. *Then* / *First*, we went to the mountains.

3a Prepare a story about a journey you had (real or invented). Think about these things:

- where you went
- who you went with
- when you went
- the transport
- the weather
- how you felt

b Work in pairs. Tell your partner about your journey. Can you guess if your partner's journey is real or invented?

## Vocabulary
### Holiday activities

**1** Match the holiday activities in the box with the pictures below.

go on a boat trip    go to the beach    go sightseeing
eat out    go shopping    visit museums
go walking    go skiing

**2a** Work in pairs. What holiday activities do you think you can do in each of these places?

1 Bariloche, Argentina
2 Florida, USA
3 Berlin, Germany
4 Coral Island, Thailand
5 Johannesburg, South Africa

**b** 🎧 11.6 Listen to five people talking about where you can do the holiday activities in exercise 1. Write which activities you can do in each place.

**3a** Think of three places you like and write down the holiday activities you can do there.

**b** Work in pairs and take turns. Ask and answer questions about what you can do in each of your places.

> I like Barcelona in Spain.
>
> Why? What can you do there?
>
> You can go to the beach, go shopping and go sightseeing …

# Task

## Interview your partner about a holiday

## Preparation Listening

**1a** Look at the photos of Tim's holiday. Can you guess the answers?

1 Where did he go on holiday last year?
2 Who did he go with?
3 How did they travel?
4 Where did they stay?
5 What did they eat?

**b** 🎧 11.7 Listen to Tim talking about his holiday and check your answers.

**2a** Listen again. Are the statements true (T) or false (F)?

1 Tim went to Rio de Janeiro in Brazil for his last holiday.
2 He went in January.
3 He went with his family.
4 They went by plane and bus.
5 They stayed in a big hotel.
6 They swam in a swimming pool.
7 They ate out in restaurants.
8 He loved his holiday.

**b** Rewrite the false statements to make them true.

**3** Listen again and tick the phrases you hear in the Useful language box.

## USEFUL LANGUAGE

**a Asking questions**

Where did you go (for your last holiday)?

When did you go (there / on holiday)?

Who did you go with?

How did you travel?

How long were you there?

Where did you stay?

What was the weather like?

What did you do there?

Did you enjoy your holiday?

**b Giving answers**

I went to (Brazil / a beach / a beautiful place).

I went (in February / two months ago / last year / in the summer).

I went with (my family / some friends / my cousin).

We went by (plane/bus/car).

We were there for (three weeks / a month).

We stayed in (a small hotel / my cousin's house).

The weather was (good/bad/hot/cold).

We (went to the beach / swam in the sea / ate out).

It was (fantastic/amazing/boring/awful)!

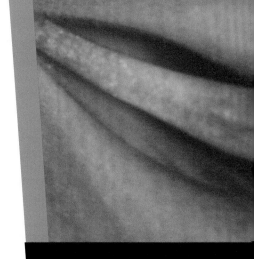

## Task Speaking

1a  Prepare to talk about a holiday or a visit to friends or family that you remember well. Make some notes, using the questions and answers in the Useful language box to help you. Ask your teacher for any words/phrases you need.

>Useful language a and b

  b  Work in pairs and take turns. Interview your partner about his/her holiday or visit. Make a note of your partner's answers.

2  Work in groups. Tell other students about your or your partner's holiday or visit.

### SHARE YOUR TASK

Practise talking about your or your partner's holiday.

Film/Record yourself talking about your or your partner's holiday.

Share your film/recording with other students.

## catch up!

**Posted: Sunday 10 a.m.**

We're here in Mumbai! We arrived at about 8 a.m. The flight from London was fine, but it was very long (9 hours on the plane)! We didn't sleep much during the flight ... we were very excited!! We watched some movies and had a nice dinner. Mumbai is a fantastic city, but it's very hot – about 35°C! We're at the hotel now, and we're very tired. We want a hot shower and a sleep!

## Writing
### A blog about a journey

**1** Read about Alisha's trip to Mumbai and answer the questions.

   1 Where did Alisha fly to?
   2 Where did she travel from?
   3 How long was the flight?
   4 Did she sleep on the plane?
   5 What is the temperature in Mumbai?
   6 Where is she now?

**2** Use the questions to make notes about a journey. (You can invent the details.)

   1 Where are you now?
   2 When did you arrive?
   3 Where did you fly from?
   4 How many hours were you on the plane?
   5 What did you do during the flight?
   6 What's the temperature where you are now?
   7 How do you feel now?
   8 What do you want to do now?

**3** Use your notes from exercise 2 to complete the gaps.

**Posted: Tuesday 2 p.m.**

We're here in ¹_____ . We arrived about ²_____ . The flight from ³_____ was fine ... about ⁴_____ hours on the plane. During the flight we ⁵_____ . ⁶_____ is a fantastic city, but it's very ⁷_____ . We're at the hotel now, and we're very ⁸_____ . We want a ⁹_____ and a ¹⁰_____ .

Return, please.

## Speaking
### Travelling by train

**1** ▶ Watch the video and choose the correct answers.

1 Laura and Alex are **at a bus stop** / **on the train** / **at the train station**.
2 The suitcase is **Alex's** / **Laura's** / **someone else's**.
3 Laura travels **alone** / **with Alex** / **with someone else**.
4 Laura buys her train ticket **at the ticket office** / **on the train** / **on the internet**.
5 The telephone call is from **Alex** / **Laura's mother** / **someone else**.

**2** Watch again and complete the details of Laura's journey.

To: _____
Leaves at: _____
Platform number: _____
Single/Return: _____
Price: _____

**3a** Which phrase didn't you hear? Tick the phrase.

• Which platform?
• Platform 3.
• What time's the next train?
• It's at 10.58 ... in one minute.
• Safe journey.
• Where to?
• Can I have a ticket to London, please?
• Single or return?
• Single.
• Return, please.
• That's £80, please.

**b** Watch again and check your answer.

---

**PRONUNCIATION**

**1** ▶ Watch and listen to the key phrases.

**2** Practise saying them.

---

**4** Complete the conversation. (You can invent information.)

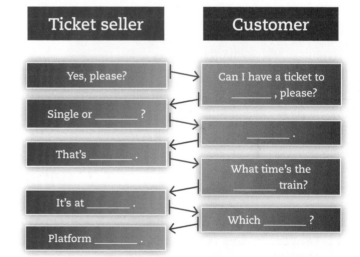

| Ticket seller | Customer |
|---|---|
| Yes, please? | Can I have a ticket to _____ , please? |
| Single or _____ ? | _____ . |
| That's _____ . | What time's the _____ train? |
| It's at _____ . | Which _____ ? |
| Platform _____ . | |

**5** Work in pairs. Student A is the ticket seller. Student B is the customer. Practise saying the conversations.

**AFTER UNIT 11 YOU CAN ...**

Ask and answer questions about journeys.

Interview someone about their holiday.

Write a short blog about a journey.

Buy a ticket and ask for information at a railway station.

# 12

## WHAT DO YOU WANT?

### IN THIS UNIT

- Grammar: *want* and *want to*; *going to*
- Vocabulary: Verb phrases about wants; Things you can buy; Describing objects: colours and sizes
- Task: Choose a present for someone you know
- Language live: Saying goodbye; Signing off

## Vocabulary
### Verb phrases about wants

**1** Match the verb phrases with the photos.

| | |
|---|---|
| go diving | perform on stage |
| travel round the world | do a course in jewellery-making |
| join a singing group | start a football team |

**2** Work in pairs and discuss.

- Which of the activities in exercise 1 do you think are:
  fun?
  boring?
  creative?
- Do you know anyone who does or did any of the activities recently? Who?

> Do you know anyone who went diving recently?

> Yes … my cousin went diving in the Red Sea last year.

## GRAMMAR

**want + noun**
I **want a cat**.
I **don't want a holiday**.
She **wants a diving holiday**.

**want to + verb**
I **want to travel** round the world.
I **don't want to travel**.
He **doesn't want to travel**.

**Questions**
What **do** you **want to** do?
**Do** you **want a** holiday? Yes, I **do**. / No, I **don't**.
**Does** he **want to** travel? Yes, he **does**. / No, he **doesn't**.

**2a** Complete the gaps with one word only.

   **1 A:** What _____ you want to do?
      **B:** I want _____ take part in a run for charity.
   **2 A:** Do you _____ to perform on stage?
      **B:** No, I _____ . I want to learn to play the guitar
        for myself.
   **3 A:** What does he _____ ?
      **B:** He wants _____ bike. He wants to cycle to
        work every day.
   **4 A:** Does she want _____ do a course?
      **B:** Yes, she _____ . She wants to learn Spanish, but
        she _____ want to do an exam.

**b** 🎧 **12.2 Listen and check.**

## PRONUNCIATION

**1** Listen again to the conversations and notice the linking
between *want to* and *want a*.

**2** Work in pairs and practise the conversations.

**3a** Think of five things you want in the next five years.
Use the ideas on page 88, on this page and your
own ideas.

**b** Work in pairs and take turns. Ask each other about
the things you want.

> What do you want to do in the next five years?
>
> > I want to do a Spanish course.

▸ Unit 12, Study & Practice 1, page 120

# Grammar focus 1
*want* and *want to*

**1a** 🎧 **12.1** Sarah and Tom got married last month.
Listen to them talking about what they want to do.
Which of the activities in the photos do they talk
about?

**b** Who says these sentences, Tom or Sarah? Listen
again and check.

   **1** I want to get a cat.
   **2** I don't want to get a cat!
   **3** I want to travel.
   **4** I don't want a holiday.

**c** Work in pairs and discuss. Do you think Tom and
Sarah are a good match?

# Vocabulary
## Things you can buy

**1a** Match the things in the pictures with the words in the table.

| Clothes | Accessories |
|---------|-------------|
| a T-shirt | earrings |
| a jacket | an umbrella |
| jeans | a watch |
| a scarf | a wallet |

**b** 🎧 **12.3** Listen and repeat the words.

**2** Work in pairs. Can you add one more item to each category?

**3** Work in pairs. Which of the things in exercises 1 and 2 do you:

1 wear?
2 carry with you?
3 have in your house?
4 usually buy online?
5 want?

**IT'S A FACT!**
Every year people leave about 80,000 umbrellas on the London Underground.

> Which of the things do you carry with you?
>
> I usually carry my wallet and an umbrella.

# Grammar focus 2
## *going to*

**1** Look at the picture of a market. What things can you buy?

*You can buy clothes – jeans and T-shirts.*

**2** Find the people in the picture who are going to do these things.

1 He's going to have a cup of coffee.
2 They're going to buy an umbrella.
3 She's going to pay for a scarf.
4 They're going to have some doughnuts.
5 He's going to speak to an assistant.
6 She's going to try on some clothes.

**3** 🎧 **12.4** Listen to four conversations from the market and complete the sentences.

1 **A:** What are you _____ to buy today?
   **B:** I'm going _____ buy a scarf because I lost my scarf last weekend.
2 **A:** _____ you going to buy those jeans?
   **B:** I don't know. I _____ going to try them on first.
3 **A:** What are you going _____ do now?
   **B:** I'm really tired so I'm going to sit down and have a cup of coffee.
4 **A:** Are you _____ to buy a watch?
   **B:** No ... I want to look, but I'm _____ going to buy one today.

## GRAMMAR

*going to + (not) going to + verb*

| + | I'm going to buy a scarf.<br>She's going to pay for that by credit card. |
|---|---|
| – | We're not going to buy them today.<br>She's not going to speak to a shop assistant. |
| ? | What are you going to do?<br>Are you going to buy those jeans? Yes, I am. /<br>No, I'm not.<br>Is he going to have a coffee? Yes, he is. / No,<br>he isn't. |

## PRONUNCIATION

**1** 🎧 **12.5 Listen to the sentences in the Grammar box.
Notice the weak form of *to*.**

I'm going to buy a scarf.

/tə/

**2** **Practise saying the sentences.**

**4a** Match the questions 1–4 with answers a–d.

**1** What are you going to do this weekend?
**2** Are you going to have a holiday this year?
**3** What are you going to do after class?
**4** Are you going to go out this evening?

**a** I'm going to have lunch.
**b** I'm going to visit friends.
**c** No, I'm going to stay in and watch TV.
**d** Yes, I'm going to stay with my sister in the USA.

**b** 🎧 **12.6 Listen and check your answers.**

**5** Work in pairs and take turns. Ask and answer the
questions in exercise 4a. Add two more similar
questions.

> What are you going to do this weekend?
>
> I'm going to cook a special meal
> for my family.

Unit 12, Study & Practice 2, page 120

## Vocabulary
### Describing objects: colours and sizes

1  🎧 12.7 **Look at the colours. Listen and repeat.**

| red | orange | yellow | green | blue |
| purple | brown | white | black | grey |

2a  🎧 12.8 **Match the sizes in the box with pictures A–D. Listen and repeat.**

large    extra-large    small    medium

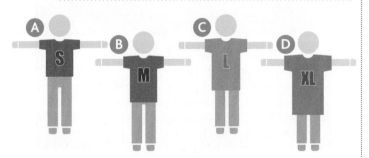

3a  🎧 12.9 **Complete the conversations with the colours and sizes. Listen and check.**

1  **A:** What colour is the T-shirt?
   **B:** It's _____ and _____ .
   **A:** What size is it?
   **B:** I think it's _____ .
2  **A:** What colour is the jacket?
   **B:** It's _____ and _____ .
   **A:** What size it is?
   **B:** I think it's _____ .
3  **A:** What colour are the umbrellas?
   **B:** They're _____ and _____ .

4  **Work in pairs and take turns. Student A: Look at the objects on page 96. Student B: Look at the objects on page 97. Ask and answer questions about the colour and size of your partner's objects.**

> What colour is the T-shirt?
>> It's green and …

# Task

## Choose a present for someone you know

### Preparation Listening

1  **Work in pairs and discuss.**

   1  In which of these situations do you usually give a present?
      • a friend's birthday
      • a friend's wedding
      • a friend has a new baby
      • a friend is ill
      • a friend has a dinner party
      • your teacher is going to leave your school
      • a colleague is going to leave your work
      • a neighbour looked after your pet while you went on holiday
   2  Can you think of any other situations when you usually give a present?

2  **Look at the examples of presents in the box. Which of them do you think are good presents for the situations in exercise 1?**

| a T-shirt | a scarf | a mug |
| some earrings | some flowers | a box of chocolates |
| a camera | a book | a voucher for a shop |

3a  🎧 12.10 **Listen to two conversations in which people are choosing presents. Answer the questions for both conversations.**

   1  Who are they choosing a present for? Why?
   2  Which presents do they think of?
   3  Which presents do they disagree about?

b  **Listen again and tick the phrases you hear in the Useful language box (parts a–c).**

4a  🎧 12.11 **Listen to two conversations about a present someone chose. Answer the questions for both conversations.**

   1  Who did they buy the present for? Why?
   2  Which present did they choose? Why?

b  **Listen again and tick the phrases you hear in the Useful language box (part d).**

**a Asking for suggestions**
What shall we take/get/buy?
Have you got any ideas?
What do you think we should get?

**b Making suggestions**
What about (a box of chocolates / some flowers)?
How about (a T-shirt / some earrings)?
We could take/get/buy (some flowers / a scarf).

**c Agreeing and disagreeing**
Yes, that's a good idea.
Yes, (he/she/everybody) likes (flowers/books).
Yes, that's a really good present.
No, (he/she) doesn't like (chocolate/reading).
No, it's difficult to buy (clothes/books) for people.
No, that's a really boring present.

**d Explaining your choice**
I'm going to give him/her (a book / some flowers).
I think it's a good present because ...
(A camera / a book) is perfect for him/her.
I/he/she suggested (a camera / a book).
But he/she doesn't like (reading).
But I'm sure they've got (a camera / a mug).

## Task Speaking

1 Work in pairs. Choose two of the situations from Preparation exercise 1. Decide together on a present for each situation. You can use the ideas from Preparation exercise 2 or your own ideas. Use the phrases in the Useful language box to help you. Ask your teacher for any words/phrases you need.

> Useful language a–c

2 Work with other students. Say which presents you chose and explain why you chose them. Use the phrases in the Useful language box to help you.

> Useful language d

**SHARE YOUR TASK**

Practise explaining which presents you chose and why.

Film/Record yourself explaining which presents you chose and why.

Share your film/recording with other students.

## Speaking
### Saying goodbye

**1** Work in pairs and discuss what people normally do in your country if someone leaves school/a job.

**2** ▶ David, Jacqui, Katy and Tim are at work. Watch the video and answer the questions.

1 Who is going to leave his/her job?
2 Is he/she happy about leaving his/her job?

**3** Watch again and choose the correct answers (a, b or c).

1 What day/time is it?
   a Monday morning
   b Thursday afternoon
   c Friday afternoon
2 Why is today special?
   a It's Katy's last day.
   b It's Tim's last day.
   c Jacqui is going to start a new job.
3 What is Katy going to do?
   a She's going to get married.
   b She's going to have a holiday.
   c She's going to live in another country.
4 What did David forget to do?
   a He forgot to buy a present for Katy.
   b He forgot to say goodbye to Katy.
   c He forgot to write a message in the card.
5 What was Katy's present?
   a jewellery
   b a T-shirt
   c a mug
6 What does Katy's text message tell her?
   a Her taxi is outside.
   b It's 5.15.
   c She's late.

**4a** Choose the correct answers.

1 *Have / Make* a nice weekend.
2 *Have / See* you on Monday!
3 *It / This* is for you.
4 *Best /Good* luck in your new job.
5 *All / Be* the best.
6 We're going to *lose / miss* you.
7 Thanks for *all / everything*.
8 *See / Watch* you again.
9 Goodbye *everybody! / all the people!*
10 *Hi! / Bye!*

**b** ▶ Watch and listen to the key phrases and check your answers.

**All the best**

**5a** Complete the conversations with the words/phrases in the box.

### Conversation 1

a nice weekend    Bye    on Monday    See you

**A:** It's 6 o'clock. It's time to go. ¹_____ tomorrow.
**B:** Tomorrow? Tomorrow's Saturday! It's the weekend!
**A:** Oh yes, I forgot. See you ²_____ .
**B:** ³_____ ! Have ⁴_____ .

### Conversation 2

for everything    for you    Good luck    miss you    the best

**C:** These are ⁵_____ . Thanks ⁶_____ .
**D:** Flowers! They're lovely! Thank you, everybody!
**C:** ⁷_____ in your new job! All ⁸_____ , Claudia!
**D:** Thank you. I'm going to ⁹_____ .

**b** Work in pairs. Choose one of the conversations and practise it. Then act it out for the rest of the class.

# Writing
## Signing off

**1** Look at the letters, emails and text messages. Which of them are formal? Which are informal?

**2** Read the letters, emails and text messages and match them with descriptions a–f.

   **a** a social network message to an old friend
   **b** a message on a leaving card
   **c** a text message to a good friend
   **d** a business letter
   **e** a message to someone you don't know very well
   **f** a business email

**Tania Harding**

**Subject:** Meeting

We can talk about any problems you have at our next meeting at 9.00 a.m. on 24th October, in the London office.
Best wishes,
Tania Harding

**catch up!**

I can send you some more photos of the holiday, if you like.
Write soon!
Give my love to Ann and the children.
Love P x

> All the best and good luck with your exams!
> James

Yours faithfully,

*Mary Procter*

**Mary Procter, Company Director**

Messages

> See you at 6 o'clock … don't be late!!!!!!!!

*Thanks for all your help.*
*Kind regards,*
*Florence W*

**3** Match the words to make phrases. Use the texts in exercise 2 to help you.

| | | | |
|---|---|---|---|
| 1 | Best | **a** | tomorrow |
| 2 | See you | **b** | faithfully |
| 3 | Kind | **c** | regards |
| 4 | Give my love | **d** | soon! |
| 5 | Good luck | **e** | to your family |
| 6 | Write | **f** | with your new job |
| 7 | Yours | **g** | wishes |

**4** Complete the message endings with suitable words.

   **1** Can't wait to hear all your news. _____ soon!   Jay
   **2** I hope to meet you again in Paris next year. _____ wishes, James Hardy
   **3** _____ on Tuesday!!!!
   **4** It was good working with you. _____ regards, Carla Stewart
   **5** _____ faithfully, Jan Havec
   **6** _____ my love to everyone in the office!   Patsy x
   **7** Good _____ in your new home!

**AFTER UNIT 12 YOU CAN …**

Talk about things you want to do.

Ask and answer questions about things you are going to do.

Choose a present for someone and say why you chose it.

Say goodbye to someone at a leaving party.

Write a formal/informal email or text message.

# Communication activities

## Unit 2: Task, Speaking

**Exercise 2, page 19**

1 Hugh Jackman is an actor. He's Australian.
2 The River Amazon is in Brazil (and also in Peru, Ecuador and Colombia).
3 Zara is a Spanish clothes company.
4 The Great Pyramid of Giza is in Egypt, near Cairo.
5 Alisher Usmanov is a Russian businessman. He is very, very rich.
6 The Shard is in London.
7 Toyota is a Japanese car company.
8 Claudia Leitte is a singer. She's Brazilian.

## Unit 6: Grammar focus 2

**Exercise 3a, page 45**

**Lola** is 27. She's a teacher – she teaches French and Spanish at a secondary school. She likes animals, but she doesn't have a pet because she travels a lot. She likes walking in the park and she goes out with her friends a lot. She also likes going to the cinema.

**Petra** is 33 and she's a waitress. She works in a Chinese restaurant. She likes her job because she likes Chinese food. She doesn't like sport and she doesn't watch TV. At the weekend, she goes to the cinema and she goes out with her friends.

## Unit 11: Grammar focus 2

**Exercise 3a, page 82**
**Student A**

You went to Vietnam and did a long bike ride. You went in November two years ago and you were there for three weeks. You did the bike ride for charity and also to see the beautiful country of Vietnam. You went with five friends. The weather was hot and sometimes it rained. You felt really tired but it was fantastic. You raised over $5,000.

## Unit 12: Vocabulary

**Exercise 4, page 92**
**Student A**
Your partner has the following items:
- a T-shirt.
- a necklace.
- a jacket.

These are your items:

# Communication activities

## Unit 10: Task, Speaking
### Exercise 1b, page 77

**Creative people quiz – answers**

1 George Lucas is a film director. He made the *Star Wars* films in the 1970s and 80s. He is also famous for directing the *Indiana Jones* films.
2 Victoria Beckham is a fashion designer. Before that, she was a member of the pop group the Spice Girls in the late 1990s. Her nickname in the band was 'Posh Spice'.
3 Gabriel García Márquez is a writer. In 1967, he wrote one of his most famous books: *One Hundred Years of Solitude*. He also wrote *Autumn of the Patriarch* and *Love in the Time of Cholera*.
4 Rudolf Nureyev was a dancer. He was born in Russia in 1938. He left Russia in 1961 and went to live in France. He died in Paris in 1993, aged 54.
5 John Lennon was a musician and a singer. He was part of the band The Beatles. He died in New York in 1980. But he wasn't from New York originally – he was from Liverpool, in the north of England.
6 Renzo Piano is an Italian architect. He designed The Shard in London. American architect Adrian Smith designed the Burj Khalifa in Dubai. British architect Richard Rogers and Spanish architect Antonio Lamela designed Terminal 4 of Madrid–Barajas Airport.
7 Gianni Versace was a fashion designer from Italy. He was born in 1946 and died in 1997. He started a fashion design business and designed clothes for many famous people.
8 J. K. Rowling is an English writer. She left Britain in 1992 and went to live in Portugal. She worked as an English teacher and started writing the *Harry Potter* books there.

## Unit 6: Grammar focus 2
### Exercise 3a, page 45

**Stefan** is 28 and he's a police officer. He works a lot, but he also likes going out with his friends. He goes to the gym and he walks in the park with his dog a lot. He likes cooking and going to restaurants. His favourite food is Spanish food.

## Unit 11: Grammar focus 2
### Exercise 3a, page 82
### Student B

You went to Europe and you cycled from London to Paris. You went in August in 2013 and you were there for ten days. You did the bike ride for charity and also to see two European capital cities, London and Paris. You went with a group of ten people. The weather was good – mostly it was warm and sunny. You felt tired, but it was really good fun. You raised about €2,000.

## Unit 12: Vocabulary
### Exercise 4, page 92
### Student B

Your partner has the following items:
- a T-shirt.
- a scarf.
- a handbag.

These are your items:

**David** is 25 and he's a student. He studies engineering at university. He plays football with his friends and he also goes to the gym a lot. He doesn't go to the cinema, but he watches a lot of TV. Mostly he watches sport – his favourite sports are football and tennis.

# 01 STUDY, PRACTICE & REMEMBER

## STUDY 1

### *I/you* and *my/your*

**Personal pronouns and possessive adjectives**

- We use personal pronouns (*I, you*) to talk about the subject of the sentence.

I                    you

- We use possessive adjectives (*my, your*) to talk about things that belong to people.

my               your

| Personal pronouns | | Possessive adjectives | |
|---|---|---|---|
| I | I'm Sonia. | my | **My** name's Gerry. |
| | I'm a teacher. | | **My** email address is p23@hotmail.com. |
| you | **You**'re an engineer. | your | **Your** first name is Nina. |
| | Are **you** Martin? | | What's **your** phone number? |

- We often use contractions when we speak.
  *I am = I'm*
  *You are = You're*

**REMEMBER!**

*I/you* (personal pronouns) + verb
*my/your* (possessive adjectives) + noun

## PRACTICE 1

**1 Choose the correct answers.**

1 **A:** Hello. What's *you / your* name?
 **B:** *My / Your* name's Alex.
2 **A:** Hi. I'm Tina. Are *you / your* Maria?
 **B:** Yes, that's right. *I / You* 'm Maria Gomez.
3 **A:** Hello. *I / My* name's Tom.
 **B:** Hi. *I / My* 'm Sam.
4 **A:** Hi. What's *your / my* name?
 **B:** *My / You* name's Peter. Nice to meet you.

**2 Complete the dialogues with *I, you, my* and *your*.**

 **A:** Hello. What's [1] ___ name?
 **B:** [2] ___ name's Chris. Are [3] ___ David?
 **A:** Yes, that's right. What's [4] ___ job?
 **B:** [5] ___ 'm an architect.

 **C:** Hi. Are [6] ___ Paula?
 **D:** Yes, that's right. What's [7] ___ name?
 **C:** [8] ___ 'm James.
 **D:** And what's [9] ___ surname?
 **C:** [10] ___ surname is Richardson.

## STUDY 2

### *a/an* with jobs

We use *a* and *an* when we talk about people's jobs. *A* and *an* are indefinite articles.

| | *an* + vowel (a, e, i, o, u) |
|---|---|
| I'm | **an a**rchitect. |
| You're | **an e**ngineer. |
| Are you | **an a**ctor? |

| | *a* + consonant (b, c, d, f ...) |
|---|---|
| I'm | **a b**usinesswoman. |
| You're | **a s**hop assistant. |
| Are you | **a t**eacher? |

**REMEMBER!**

**NOT** *You're engineer.*   **NOT** *I'm businesswoman.*   **NOT** *Are you student?*

## PRACTICE 2

**1 Choose the correct answers.**

1 I'm *a / an* businessman.
2 Are you *a / an* actor?
3 I'm *a / an* engineer.
4 I'm *a / an* shop assistant.
5 Are you *a / an* architect?
6 I'm *a / an* student.
7 Are you *a / an* teacher?
8 Are you *a / an* accountant?

**2 Write *a* or *an* in the correct place.**

I'm teacher. *I'm a teacher.*
1 You're student.
2 I'm architect.
3 Are you shop assistant?
4 I'm businessman.
5 You're engineer.
6 Are you actor?
7 I'm accountant.
8 You're businesswoman.

## STUDY 3

### The alphabet and 'How do you spell ... ?'

Aa Bb Cc Dd Ee Ff Gg Hh Ii Jj Kk Ll Mm Nn Oo Pp Qq Rr Ss Tt Uu Vv Ww Xx Yy Zz

There are 26 letters in the English alphabet. Notice the pronunciation of all the letters.

| Letters | Pronunciation |
|---------|---------------|
| a h j k | /eɪ/ |
| b c d e g p t v | /iː/ |
| f l m n s x z | /e/ |
| i y | /aɪ/ |
| o | /əʊ/ |
| q u w | /uː/ |
| r | /ɑː/ |

A: *How do you spell 'engineer'?*
B: *E-N-G-I-N-E-E-R.*
A: *What's your email address?*
B: *steve.price@yahoo.com*
A: *How do you spell that?*
B: *S-T-E-V-E-dot-P-R-I-C-E-@-Y-A-H-O-O-dot-com*

## PRACTICE 3

### 1 Say the answers.

1  How do you spell 'teacher'?
2  How do you spell your surname?
3  How do you spell your email address?
4  How do you spell 'businessman'?
5  How do you spell 'eighteen'?
6  How do you spell your first name?
7  How do you spell 'accountant'?
8  How do you spell 'twelve'?

## REMEMBER THESE WORDS

**JOBS**

| | |
|---|---|
| accountant | businessman/businesswoman |
| actor | shop assistant |
| architect | student |
| engineer | teacher |

**NUMBERS 0–20**

| | | | | | |
|---|---|---|---|---|---|
| 0 | zero | 7 | seven | 14 | fourteen |
| 1 | one | 8 | eight | 15 | fifteen |
| 2 | two | 9 | nine | 16 | sixteen |
| 3 | three | 10 | ten | 17 | seventeen |
| 4 | four | 11 | eleven | 18 | eighteen |
| 5 | five | 12 | twelve | 19 | nineteen |
| 6 | six | 13 | thirteen | 20 | twenty |

**OTHER**

| | | |
|---|---|---|
| name | alphabet | hello |
| first name | spell | goodbye |
| surname | job | How are you? |
| number | town | I'm fine. |
| phone number | school | Nice to meet you! |
| email address | workplace | See you again! |

## PRACTICE

### 1 Add letters to complete the jobs and numbers.

1  t_ac_er           5  b_s_n_ss_an
2  e_g_t             6  fi_t_e_
3  _n_ineer          7  ar_h_t_ct
4  el_ _en           8  t_ _ _ty

### 2 Look at the words in 1 again. How do you spell them? Say the letters.

*How do you spell 'teacher'?*
*T-E-A-C-H-E-R.*

### 3 Complete the sentences with the words from the box.

surname  first  spell  How  fine  meet  again  address

1  What's your _____ name?
2  How do you _____ your name?
3  Nice to _____ you!
4  What's your email _____ ?
5  _____ are you?
6  I'm _____ thanks.
7  My _____ is Gomez.
8  See you _____ !

### 4 Write the numbers.

| | | | | | |
|---|---|---|---|---|---|
| 2 | *two* | 19 | _____ | 8 | _____ |
| 3 | _____ | 4 | _____ | 15 | _____ |
| 7 | _____ | 20 | _____ | 13 | _____ |
| 11 | _____ | 12 | _____ | | |

## STUDY 1

### *be* with *I, you, he/she/it*

**+ Positive**

| | |
|---|---|
| I'm (= I am) | I'm from Spain. |
| You're (= You are) | You're Italian. |
| He's (= he is) | He's a student. |
| She's (= she is) | She's twenty-three. |
| It's (= It is) | It's in London. |

**– Negative**

| | |
|---|---|
| I'm not (= am not) | I'm not from Spain. |
| You're not *or* You aren't (= are not) | You're not French. You aren't a doctor. |
| He isn't (= is not) | He isn't from Russia. |
| She isn't (= is not) | She isn't fifty. |
| It isn't (= is not) | It isn't in Washington. |

**? Questions**

| | |
|---|---|
| Am I ... ? | Am I late? |
| Are you ...? | Where are you from? |
| Is he ... ? | Is he French? |
| Is she ... ? | Is she from Spain? |
| Is it ... ? | Is it a big city? |

We often use contractions when we speak.
*I'm / I'm not*
*You're / You're not* (or *You aren't*)
*He's / He isn't*
*She's / She isn't*
*It's / It isn't*

## PRACTICE 1

**1 Choose the correct answers.**

1 I *'m* / *'re* from Brazil.
2 You *'m* / *'re* a teacher.
3 *Are* / *Is* you from Egypt?
4 He *'re* / *'s* an accountant.
5 *Are* / *Is* she from the USA?
6 Where *are* / *is* you from?
7 He *aren't* / *isn't* a student.
8 You *'m* / *'re* not from England.

**2 Complete the sentences with the words from the box.**

| am | am | is | is | isn't | isn't | are | are | are | aren't |

1 Where _____ you from?
2 No, you _____ a teacher.
3 _____ he Spanish?
4 No, she _____ thirty-one.
5 Yes, I _____ twenty-three.
6 Where _____ the River Thames.
7 No, I _____ not from Australia.
8 _____ you from Vietnam?
9 No, he _____ from Portugal.
10 _____ you a student?

**3 Rewrite the sentences to make questions.**

He's French.
*Is he French?*

1 You're from London.
   _____
2 It's a big city.
   _____
3 I'm late for school.
   _____
4 She's a teacher.
   _____
5 You're thirty years old.
   _____
6 I'm a student.
   _____
7 He's from Brazil.
   _____
8 You're Japanese.
   _____

## STUDY 2

### *his/her*

We use possessive adjectives (*his*, *her*) to talk about things that belong to people.

| Possessive adjectives | |
|---|---|
| his | His name's Michael. |
| | His email address is michaelp@hotmail.com. |
| | What's his job? |
| her | Her first name's Jane. |
| | Her family name's Smith. |
| | What's her phone number? |

**REMEMBER!**

*his/her/my/your* (possessive adjectives) + noun
**His name's** James.
*What's **your phone number?***

*I/you/he/she* (personal pronouns) + verb
**He is** a teacher.
**I'm** from Australia.

## PRACTICE 2

**1 Complete the sentences with *His* or *Her*.**

1 He's a doctor. _____ name's David.
2 She's from Spain. _____ name's Gabriela.
3 He's from England. _____ name's Steve.
4 He's an engineer. _____ name's James.
5 She's a teacher. _____ name's Marianna.
6 She's from Russia. _____ name's Olga.
7 He's from the USA. _____ name's Tom.
8 She's an accountant. _____ name's Sarah.

**2 Choose the correct answers.**

1 My teacher is from England. ***His* / *He*** name's Jon.
2 Anne is from Australia. ***Her* / *She*** surname's Cooper.
3 My teacher's name is Robert. ***His* / *He*** is from the USA.
4 Maria is a student. ***Her* / *She's*** from Spain.
5 Anton is from Russia. ***His* / *He*** email address is ant@gmail.com.
6 ***Her* / *She*** phone number is 07789 456887.
7 My friend's name is Julia. ***Her* / *She*** is nineteen.
8 Roberto is a student. ***His* / *He's*** Italian.

**3 Read the information and complete the sentences about Maria and Steve.**

| 1 | First name | Maria |
|---|---|---|
| 2 | Surname | Gomez |
| 3 | Phone number | 07343 221665 |
| 4 | Country | Spain |
| 5 | Nationality | Spanish |

| 6 | First name | Steve |
|---|---|---|
| 7 | Surname | Johnson |
| 8 | Phone number | 646 896 3342 |
| 9 | Country | USA |
| 10 | Nationality | American |

1 *Her first name's Maria.*          6 *His first name's Steve.*
2 _____          7 _____
3 _____          8 _____
4 _____          9 _____
5 _____          10 _____

### REMEMBER THESE WORDS

**COUNTRIES AND NATIONALITIES**

Australia – Australian
Brazil – Brazilian
China – Chinese
Egypt – Egyptian
England – English
Italy – Italian
Japan – Japanese
Russia – Russian

Vietnam – Vietnamese
United States of America (USA) – American
Portugal – Portuguese
Argentina – Argentinian
Spain – Spanish
Poland – Polish

**NUMBERS 21-100**

| | | |
|---|---|---|
| 21 twenty-one | 28 twenty-eight | 40 forty |
| 22 twenty-two | 29 twenty-nine | 50 fifty |
| 23 twenty-three | 30 thirty | 60 sixty |
| 24 twenty-four | 31 thirty-one | 70 seventy |
| 25 twenty-five | 32 thirty-two | 80 eighty |
| 26 twenty-six | ... | 90 ninety |
| 27 twenty-seven | | 100 a hundred |

**OTHER**

| | | |
|---|---|---|
| pizza | a place | I'm fifty. |
| tortilla | a person | age |
| samba music | people | I think ... |
| a river | winner | I don't know. |
| a (clothes/car) company | How old are you? | best friend |

## PRACTICE

**1 Write the missing countries and nationalities.**

1 I'm from Brazil. I'm _____ .
2 She's from Russia. She's _____ .
3 He's from _____ . He's English.
4 I'm from Egypt. I'm _____ .
5 You're from Portugal. You're _____ .
6 She's from _____ . She's Italian.
7 I'm from China. I'm _____ .
8 He's from _____ . He's Spanish.

**2 Mark the stress on the countries and nationalities.**

Portugal – Portuguese

1 China – Chinese
2 Brazil – Brazilian
3 Poland – Polish
4 Italy – Italian
5 Japan – Japanese
6 Egypt – Egyptian
7 Australia – Australian
8 England – English

**3 Choose the correct answers.**

1 A: How ***old* / *age*** is she?
   B: She's twenty-five.
2 A: Where is samba music from?
   B: I ***am* / *think*** it's from Brazil.
3 A: What's Chevrolet?
   B: It's an American car ***country* / *company***.
4 A: Where is the River Nile?
   B: I don't ***think* / *know***.
5 A: How old are you?
   B: I ***old* / *am*** thirty-nine.
6 A: Who is Daniela?
   B: She's my best ***person* / *friend***.

**4 Write the numbers.**

| 29 | *twenty-nine* | 99 | _____ | 100 | _____ |
|---|---|---|---|---|---|
| 43 | _____ | 81 | _____ | 74 | _____ |
| 38 | _____ | 25 | _____ | 58 | _____ |
| 62 | _____ | 57 | _____ | | |

## STUDY 1

### this/that, these/those

**REMEMBER!**

We use *this* and *that* with singular nouns and *these* and *those* with plural nouns.

| **this** car | **these** cars |
| **that** shop | **those** shops |

## PRACTICE 1

**1 Choose the correct answers.**

1 A: *This / These* is my friend, Daniel.
   B: Nice to meet you!
2 A: Are *that / those* people your teachers?
   B: Yes, he's American and she's English.
3 A: Are *this / these* vegetables good?
   B: Yes ... delicious!
4 A: Is *that / those* bread nice?
   B: Yes, it is.
5 A: *This / These* is my email address.
   B: Thank you.
6 A: *This / These* apples are very cheap.
   B: Yes, and very nice!
7 A: *That / Those* shops are expensive.
   B: Yes ... very expensive!
8 A: Is *that / those* sandwich nice?
   B: No, it isn't.

**2 Complete the sentences with *this*, *that*, *these* or *those*.**

1 _____ is my book.

2 Who are _____ people?

3 Look at _____ cakes!

4 _____ is my dog.

5 _____ are my children.

6 Look at _____ car!

7 _____ is my sandwich.

8 Are _____ your keys?

## STUDY 2

### be with we and they

**+ Positive**

| **we're** (= we are) | **We're** from Spain. |
| **they're** (= they are) | **They're** in New York. |

**– Negative**

| **we're not** or **we aren't** (= are not) | **We aren't** very happy. |
| **they're not** or **they aren't** (= are not) | **They aren't** expensive. |

**? Questions**

| **are we** ... ? | **Are we** in Argentina? |
| **are they** ... ? | Where **are they** from? |

We often use contractions when we speak.

*We're / We're not* or *We aren't*
*They're / They're not* or *They aren't*

## PRACTICE 2

**1 Put the words in the correct order to make sentences and questions.**

1 Spain / are / We / from .
2 aren't / They / happy .
3 from / Are / Brazil / they ?
4 are / They / teachers .
5 students / aren't / We .
6 expensive / they / Are ?
7 the UK / aren't / They / from .
8 in / We / Italy / are .

**2 Student A: Write negative sentences.**

We are in Japan. *We aren't in Japan.*
1 We are students.
2 They are from China.
3 Linda and Kim are accountants.
4 We are happy.
5 We are in Italy.
6 Those potatoes are cheap.

**Student B: Write questions.**

They are teachers. *Are they teachers?*
1 They are Australian.
2 We are in a Japanese restaurant.
3 Those sandwiches are awful.
4 They are expensive.
5 We are in London.
6 David and Nicky are on holiday.

## REMEMBER THESE WORDS

**PLURAL NOUNS**

| | |
|---|---|
| shop – shops | city – cities |
| taxi – taxis | country – countries |
| car – cars | nationality – nationalities |
| student – students | man – men |
| bus – buses | woman – women |
| address – addresses | person – people |
| sandwich – sandwiches | child – children |

**ADJECTIVES – OPPOSITES**

| | |
|---|---|
| friendly | happy |
| unfriendly | sad |
| cheap | fantastic |
| expensive | awful |

**FOOD AND DRINK**

| | |
|---|---|
| tea | apples |
| coffee | vegetables |
| milk | potatoes |
| water | bread |
| meat | rice |
| fish | pasta |
| chicken | eggs |
| fruit | cheese |

**OTHER**

| | |
|---|---|
| on holiday | delicious |
| on business | horrible |
| hotel | breakfast |
| capital city | the same as |
| official language | different from |
| colours | typical |
| black | favourite |
| white | |
| red | |
| yellow | |

## PRACTICE

**1 Write the plural nouns.**

1 taxi – _____
2 sandwich – _____
3 country – _____
4 woman – _____
5 bus – _____
6 city – _____
7 person – _____
8 child – _____

**2 Put the words from the box into the correct category.**

cheese   coffee   white   tea   man   apples   black
milk   child   yellow   chicken   woman

1 Food: _____ , _____ and _____
2 Drinks: _____ , _____ and _____
3 People: _____ , _____ and _____
4 Colours: _____ , _____ and _____

**3 Complete the sentences using words from the box.**

expensive   holiday   delicious   vegetables   milk
friendly   yellow   meat

1 My favourite _____ are potatoes.
2 £15! This sandwich is very _____ !
3 Taxis in my country are red and _____ .
4 Chicken is my favourite kind o _____ .
5 My typical breakfast is black coffee ... that's with no
_____ .
6 The people in my city are very _____ .
7 This pasta is fantastic! Mmm, _____ !
8 We are in Spain on _____ . I'm happy!

## STUDY 1

### Prepositions of place

We use prepositions of place to talk about where things are.

The café is **on the left of** the hotel.

The lake is **in** the park.

The hotel is **on the right of** the café.

The people are **near** the bus stop.

---

**REMEMBER!**

**NOT** *The people are near of the bus stop.*
**NOT** *The hotel is near of the park.*

## PRACTICE 1

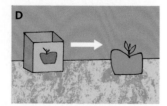

**1 Match the sentences (1–4) with the pictures (A–D).**

1 The apple is on the right of the box.
2 The apple is in the box.
3 The apple is on the left of the box.
4 The apple is near the box.

**2 Underline the one or two correct words.**

1 The train station is *in / left / near* the hotel.
2 The supermarket is on the *left / right / near* of the cinema.
3 The man is *in / right / near* his car.
4 My sandwich is *left / near / in* my bag.
5 The school is on the *left / near / right* of the train station.
6 My house is *near / in / right* the beach.
7 The café is *left / right / in* the park.
8 The post office is on the *near / left / right* of the bank.

## STUDY 2

### *there is* and *there are*

| Singular |
| --- |
| **There's** a hotel on the left of the train station. |
| **There's** an island near my town. |

| Plural |
| --- |
| **There are** three women near the bus stop. |
| **There are** fifteen cafés in my town. |

We often use contractions when we speak, but only in the singular form (**NOT** in the plural form).
*There is a hotel. / There's a hotel.*
*There are three cafés.* **NOT** *There're three cafés.*

## PRACTICE 2

**1 Choose the correct answers.**

1 There *is / are* an old man in the café.
2 There *is / are* three buses at the bus stop.
3 There *is / are* ten people near the post office.
4 There *is / are* a child with the woman.
5 There *is / are* a big cinema in my town.
6 There *is / are* two men in the restaurant.
7 There *is / are* an expensive restaurant near the train station.
8 There *is / are* three children in the car.

**2 Complete the sentences with *There's* and *There are*.**

1 _____ a car park near the station.
2 _____ five people in that taxi.
3 _____ one hotel in my town.
4 _____ two Italian restaurants in this street.
5 _____ three women in the sea.
6 _____ an old university in my town.
7 _____ a river near my house.
8 _____ eleven parks in my city.

## STUDY 3

### *there is* and *there are* positive, negative and questions

- We use *a/an* in positive, singular sentences.
- We use *some* and *a lot of* in positive, plural sentences.
- We use *a/an* in negative, singular sentences.
- We use *any* in negative, plural sentences.
- We use *a/an* in singular questions.
- We use *any* in plural questions.

|  | Singular | Plural |
|---|---|---|
| + | **There's a** car park near the station. | **There are some** hotels.<br>**There are a lot of** beaches. |
| - | **There isn't a** cinema in our town.<br>**There isn't a** station here. | **There aren't any** restaurants.<br>**There aren't any** people here. |
| ? | **Is there a** post office in this street?<br>**Is there an** island near your town? | **Are there any** shops here?<br>**Are there any** beaches near here? |
| Short answers | Yes, **there is.**<br>No, **there isn't.** | Yes, **there are.**<br>No, **there aren't.** |

## PRACTICE 3

**1 Choose the correct words.**

1 There is *a / some* cinema on the left of the hotel.
2 There are *some / any* islands near the beach.
3 Is there *a / any* train station near here?
4 There aren't *some / any* buses to my town.
5 There isn't *some / a* good beach in this town.
6 Are there *any / some* people on that bus?
7 There are *a lot of / any* children here.
8 There aren't *any / some* cheap hotels here.

**2 Complete the sentences with *a/an*, *some* or *any*.**

1 There is _____ expensive restaurant near my house.
2 There are _____ fantastic parks in London.
3 Is there _____ pen in your bag?
4 Are there _____ good shops near here?
5 There isn't _____ bank in this street.
6 There aren't _____ chairs in here.
7 Is there _____ café in your school?
8 Are there _____ good restaurants near here?

**PLACES IN A TOWN**

| | | |
|---|---|---|
| a café | a supermarket | a square |
| a restaurant | a bank | a park |
| a cinema | a bus stop | a car park |
| a hotel | a train station | a shopping centre |

**NATURAL FEATURES**

| | | | |
|---|---|---|---|
| the sea | a lake | an island | a mountain |
| a beach | a river | a hill | a rainforest |

**OTHER**

| | | | |
|---|---|---|---|
| eat | town/city centre | fantastic | big |
| travel | cathedral | beautiful | small |
| buy (food) | university | great | old |
| get (money) | street | good | |
| meet (friends) | famous | nice | |

## PRACTICE

**1 Put the words and phrases in the box into the correct category.**

train station   mountain   supermarket   café   school
lake   bus stop   university   hill   restaurant   river
shopping centre

1 Places to eat: _____
2 Places to go on a boat: _____
3 Places to get transport: _____
4 Places to buy things: _____
5 Places to study: _____
6 Places to walk up: _____

**2 Are these sentences true or false for you? Make the false sentences correct.**

1 There's a park near my school/work.
2 There's a café near my house.
3 There are two train stations in my town.
4 There's a beach in my town.
5 There are two mountains near my town.
6 There's an Italian restaurant in the shopping centre in my town.
7 There's a river in my town.
8 There are three cinemas in my town.

**3 Add vowels (*a, e, i, o* and *u*) to complete the adjectives.**

gr _ _ t  *great*
1 b _ g
2 sm _ ll
3 _ ld
4 g _ _ d
5 n _ c _
6 f _ m _ _ s
7 f _ nt _ st _ c
8 b _ _ _ t _ f _ l

**4 Write two things with each adjective in exercise 3.**

*a great hotel; a great man*

## STUDY 1

### Possessive 's

Tara is Antonio's wife.
Gina's grandmother is 96.

That is Steve's car.
Emiko is Jun and Aya's daughter.

**REMEMBER!**
**NOT** Tara is the wife of Antonio.
**NOT** That is the car of Steve.

| 's = possessive | AND | 's = is |
|---|---|---|
| Tom is Linda's father. | | Linda's a student. |
| This is Jim's car. | | She's from Brazil. |

## PRACTICE 1

**1 Look at the words in bold. Write an apostrophe (')
where necessary.**

Jane is **Tom's** sister.
My **teachers** are David and Sarah.
1 Danny is **Bens** brother.
2 My **sisters** name is Debbie.
3 There are two **cinemas** in my town.
4 The **companys** name is Morgan and Co.
5 Tom is **Dianas** husband.
6 Their **names** are Tina and Gaby.
7 My **brothers** name is Mario.
8 My **teachers** name is Tony.

**2 Write the possessive 's in the correct place in each sentence.**

Daniel is David brother. *Daniel is David's brother.*
1 Rosa is Marian mother.
2 My brother name is Jaime.
3 Lara and Ben are Kim parents.
4 My teacher name is Jane Johnson.
5 Luisa is Carmen daughter.
6 My friend name is Simone.
7 Tom and Jack are my sister children.
8 Nico is Sandra husband.

## STUDY 2

### Present simple (I, you, we, they)

| + Positive | − Negative (don't + verb) |
|---|---|
| I **live** in Japan.<br>You **work** in a small company.<br>We **have** three children.<br>They **study** Engineering. | I **don't study** Spanish.<br>You **don't have** a car.<br>We **don't go** to work by bus.<br>They **don't live** in the town centre. |

## PRACTICE 2

**1 Choose the correct answers.**

1 They *live / go* in a big house in Madrid.
2 I *speak / study* engineering at university.
3 My children *go / have* to school in the town centre.
4 We *don't speak / don't work* in an office.
5 They *speak / have* English, Spanish and French.
6 I *don't have / don't work* any children.
7 You *live / work* as a teacher in a school.
8 They *go / live* in a flat with their parents.

**2 Complete the sentences with the verbs in the box.**

go  have  study  teach  don't have  don't live
don't speak  don't work

1 I _____ three brothers and one sister.
2 I live in a flat. I _____ in a house.
3 I'm a teacher. I _____ business at university.
4 I _____ a job – I'm a student.
5 There are thirty students in my class. We _____ English.
6 My parents work in a hospital. They _____ to work by bus.
7 I _____ in an office – I work in a school.
8 My parents speak Spanish but they _____ English.

## STUDY 3

### Present simple questions (I, you, we, they)

**A Yes/No questions**

| Do | subject | verb | ... |
|---|---|---|---|
| **Do** | I | **go** | by bus? |
| **Do** | you | **speak** | Japanese? |
| **Do** | we | **study** | English? |
| **Do** | they | **live** | in a flat? |

**Short answers**

*Do you live in a flat?*
*Yes, I do. No, I don't.*          **NOT** *Yes, I live. No, I don't live.*

**B Wh- questions**

| question word | do | subject | verb | ... |
|---|---|---|---|---|
| Where | **do** | I | **go?** | |
| Where | **do** | you | **live?** | |
| What | **do** | we | **study** | at school? |
| Who | **do** | they | **live** | with? |

**1 Match the questions (1–8) with the answers (a–h).**

1 Do you go to work by bus?
2 What languages do they study?
3 Do you have any children?
4 Where do they live?
5 Where do you work?
6 Do you live in a big house?
7 Who do you live with?
8 Do you have a cat?

a No, I don't. I live in a flat.
b Yes, I do ... two daughters.
c My parents and my sister.
d English and Chinese.
e No, I don't. I go by train.
f No, I don't, but I have two dogs.
g In Osaka, a city in Japan.
h In a school. I'm a teacher.

**2 Complete the questions using the words in brackets.**

1 Where _____ (you/live)?
2 What languages _____ (they/speak)?
3 _____ (you/go) to school by train?
4 _____ (they/live) in the town centre?
5 Where _____ (we/work)?
6 _____ (you/have) any children?
7 Who _____ (they/work) with?
8 What _____ (you/study) at university?

## REMEMBER THESE WORDS

**FAMILY**

| | |
|---|---|
| husband | brother |
| wife | sister |
| parents | grandparents |
| father | grandfather |
| mother | grandmother |
| children | grandchildren |
| son | grandson |
| daughter | granddaughter |

**VERBS WITH NOUN PHRASES**

| | | |
|---|---|---|
| go to school | live in a flat | work in an office |
| go home for lunch | live with your family | work for a big |
| go to work by bus | live in a house | company |
| have children | study medicine | work in a team of |
| have a car | study at university | people |
| have two brothers | study languages | |

**OTHER**

| | | | |
|---|---|---|---|
| medicine | business | speak | at the weekend |
| engineering | teach | alone | magazine |

## PRACTICE

**1 Put the words in the box into the correct category.**

~~father~~ children  parents  brother  wife  grandparents
mother  grandchildren  daughter  sister  husband  son

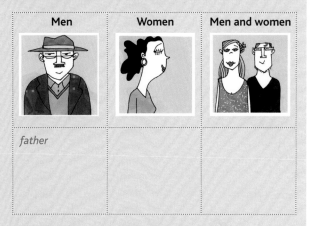

| Men | Women | Men and women |
|---|---|---|
| father | | |

**2 Rewrite the sentences to make them true for you.**

1 I have two brothers.
2 I live with my parents.
3 I work with children.
4 My grandparents live near me.
5 My sister's husband is American.
6 I have a son and a daughter.
7 My children study at university.
8 My mother is a teacher.

**3 Complete the sentences with a verb from the box.**

go  have  live  go  work  study  work  study

1 They _____ in an office.
2 I _____ with my family in the town centre.
3 Do you _____ at university?
4 We _____ three brothers.
5 Do you _____ to work by bus?
6 Do they _____ for a big company?
7 I _____ home for lunch.
8 Where do you _____ English?

**4 Choose the correct answers.**

1 I go home *for / by* lunch.
2 They go to work *by / with* bus.
3 We live *in / at* a flat.
4 Do you study *at / by* university?
5 I work *at / for* a big company.
6 They play football *for / at* the weekend.
7 Do you live *by / with* your family?
8 I go *at / to* school every day.

# 06 STUDY, PRACTICE & REMEMBER

## STUDY 1

### Present simple (*he, she, it*)

| + Positive | – Negative (*doesn't* + verb) |
|---|---|
| He **likes** football a lot. | He **doesn't like** watching TV. |
| **My brother lives** in Poland. | Alex **doesn't live** in Spain. |
| **She works** with children. | She **doesn't play** tennis. |
| **Debbie reads** a lot of magazines. | Maryam **doesn't use** a laptop. |
| **My town has** a cinema. | It **doesn't have** a shopping centre. |

- Most verbs: add *-s*
  *work* → *works*    *live* → *lives*
- Verbs ending in *-ch*, *-sh* or *-o*:  add *-es*
  *watch* → *watches*   *go* → *goes*
- Verbs that end in *-y*: *-y* → *-ies*
  *study* → *studies*
- Irregular form:
  *have* → *has*

### REMEMBER!

We use *doesn't* + verb (infinitive) in the negative form (NOT *doesn't* + Present simple form)

*He **doesn't live** in Spain.* **NOT** *He doesn't lives in Spain.*
*She **doesn't have** a dog.* **NOT** *She doesn't has a dog.*
*My TV **doesn't work**.* **NOT** *My TV doesn't works.*

## PRACTICE 1

**1 Look at the verbs in bold and add -s or -es or nothing (x).**

Simon live in the town centre.
*Simon lives in the town centre.*

1 James **like** jazz music.
2 My sisters **love** going to the cinema.
3 Her brother **watch** TV a lot.
4 I **use** a computer when I'm at work.
5 She **read** a newspaper every day.
6 Stella **teach** English at university.
7 You **go** to the gym every day.
8 Martin **work** in a big office.

**2 Rewrite the sentences using the negative form of the verbs.**

1 David likes playing tennis.
2 My sister goes to school in the town centre.
3 My school has a big library.
4 Maria studies medicine at university.
5 My brother reads a lot of computer magazines.
6 Jenny lives near the beach.
7 My town has a lot of interesting cafés.
8 My cousin goes to the USA every year.

## STUDY 2

### Present simple questions (*he, she, it*)

| Does | subject | verb | ... |
|---|---|---|---|
| **Does** | he | **like** | cats? |
| **Does** | your brother | **live** | in Italy? |
| **Does** | she | **eat** | meat? |
| **Does** | Monica | **go** | to school by car? |
| **Does** | your town | **have** | a cinema? |
| **Does** | it | **have** | a shopping centre? |
| **Short answers** | | | |
| *Yes, he/she/it does. No, he/she/it doesn't.*<br>NOT *Yes she likes.* | | | |

### REMEMBER!

We use *does/doesn't* in short answers (**NOT** ~~the Present simple form~~)
*Yes, she does.* **NOT** *Yes, she likes.*
*No, he doesn't.* **NOT** *No, he doesn't like.*

## PRACTICE 2

**1a Circle the correct answers.**

1 ***Do / Does*** you eat meat?
2 ***Do / Does*** your brother use a laptop?
3 ***Do / Does*** Sarah live near you?
4 ***Do / Does*** your parents have a car?
5 ***Do / Does*** your teacher speak Chinese?
6 ***Do / Does*** your town have a train station?
7 ***Do / Does*** you study at university?
8 ***Do / Does*** your sister live with you?

**b Write answers for the questions in exercise 1a, starting with the words given.**

1 Yes, _____     5 Yes, _____
2 No, _____      6 No, _____
3 No, _____      7 Yes, _____
4 Yes, _____     8 Yes, _____

**2 Write questions and short answers from the sentences.**

Mark doesn't live with his family.
*Does Mark live with his family? No, he doesn't.*

1 James plays tennis every Saturday.
2 Your brother doesn't live with you.
3 His teacher goes to work by car.
4 Your town has a big swimming pool.
5 She doesn't eat meat.
6 Soraya likes going to the cinema.
7 He doesn't speak French.
8 Cassia doesn't study at university.

**3 Write questions and answers about Mark and Louise.**

Mark:

1  _Does Mark play tennis?_

2  _____

3  _____

4  _____

Louise:

5  _____

6  _____

7  _____

8  _____

# PRACTICE

**1 Complete the sentences with verbs and verb phrases from the box.**

cooks   plays   uses   goes to   goes out with   reads
listens to   watches

1  My brother _____ football on TV a lot.
2  My mother _____ dinner every day.
3  Lois _____ the gym after work.
4  My teacher _____ a computer in the classroom a lot.
5  She _____ music on her MP3 player.
6  He _____ a magazine on the train.
7  Judith _____ her friends every weekend.
8  My sister _____ tennis on Saturdays.

**2 Add the vowels (a, e, i, o and u) to complete the words.**

Sports:
1  f _ _ tb _ ll
2  b _ sk _ tb _ ll
Food:
3  j _ nk f _ _ d
4  _ nd _ _ n f _ _ d
Music:
5  j _ zz
6  r _ ck m _ s _ c
Animals:
7  d _ g
8  c _ t
Physical activities:
9  r _ nn _ ng
10  d _ nc _ ng
Musical instruments:
11  g _ _ t _ r
12  p _ _ n _

**3 Write sentences about you using the words.**

like / playing football. _I don't like playing football._

1  have / pets
2  go / running
3  play / a musical instrument
4  listen to / jazz music
5  like / chicken curry
6  use / a laptop
7  watch / TV every day
8  read / a lot of magazines

## STUDY 1

### Frequency adverbs

We use frequency adverbs to talk about how often we do things. Look at the frequency adverbs on the line.

| never | don't usually | sometimes | usually | always |
|---|---|---|---|---|
| 0% | | | | 100% |
| | 25% | 50% | 75% | |

When we use frequency adverbs, the word order is: subject + adverb + verb.

| subject | adverb | verb | |
|---|---|---|---|
| I | always | have | coffee for breakfast. |
| You | usually | go | to the cinema at the weekend. |
| My sister | sometimes | plays | tennis on Sundays. |
| Children in England | don't usually | go | to school on Saturdays. |
| Japanese people | never | wear | shoes in the house. |

## PRACTICE 1

**1 Write the words in the correct order.**

1 gets up / early / He / always.
2 eat meat / You / don't usually.
3 watch TV / in the evening / never / I.
4 goes to work / sometimes / She / by bus.
5 usually / They / on Fridays / go out.
6 have breakfast / I / on weekdays / don't usually.
7 We / play football / on Sundays / always.
8 She / for her birthday / never / has a party.

**2 Add the correct frequency adverbs to the sentences.**

He goes to school by bus. (100%)
*He always goes to school by bus.*
1 She has breakfast. (0%)
2 My brother plays football at the weekend. (50%)
3 We go on holiday to the beach. (100%)
4 They have coffee after dinner. (25%)
5 I do my homework in the library. (75%)
6 He goes to the gym on Saturdays. (100%)
7 I work late on Fridays. (0%)
8 They watch the football on TV. (50%)

**3 Rewrite the sentences using frequency adverbs to make them true for you.**

I have breakfast. *I never have breakfast.*
1 I have lunch at home.
2 I get up before 7 a.m.
3 I watch TV in the evening.
4 I go to the gym on Saturdays.
5 I go to the beach on holiday.
6 I have coffee for breakfast.
7 I work late on Fridays.
8 I go to bed after 11 p.m.

## STUDY 2

### Present simple *Wh-* questions

Question words:
· *what* asks about a thing
· *who* asks about a person
· *where* asks about a place
· *when* asks about a time
· *why* asks about a reason
· *how many* asks about a number

The word order with *Wh-* questions is different for different verbs.

**A with verb *be*: question word + verb *be* + subject**

| Question word | verb *be* | subject |
|---|---|---|
| What | are | those? |
| Who | is | that? |
| Where | are | your parents? |
| When | is | the party? |

**B with other verbs: question word + *do/does* + subject + verb**

| Question word | *do/does* | subject | verb | |
|---|---|---|---|---|
| What | does | she | like | doing on Sundays? |
| Who | do | you | live | with? |
| Where | does | he | work? | |
| When | does | he | finish | work? |
| Why | do | they | go | by train? |
| How many children | do | you | have? | |

## PRACTICE 2

**1 Write questions using the prompts.**

1 Where _____ (you/live)?
2 What _____ (they/have) for breakfast?
3 Why _____ (you/be) late?
4 Where _____ (your brother/live)?
5 Who _____ (you/play) football with?
6 When _____ (the first class/be)?
7 How many languages _____ (you/speak)?
8 Who _____ (that man/be)?

**2 Write questions about the underlined words.**

He lives in Australia. *Where does he live?*
1 She goes to the cinema on Fridays.
2 I get up at 7 o'clock.
3 He plays tennis because it's fun.
4 They live with their parents.
5 She has four children.
6 He goes out with friends after work.
7 I work in a school.
8 She finishes work at 6:30.

**3** Read the text and answer the questions about Julia.

My name's Julia and I live with my husband in Australia. I'm a teacher in a secondary school. From Monday to Friday, I always get up at 6:30. I usually have coffee and toast for breakfast. I go to work at 7:45 and start work at 9 o'clock. I sometimes have lunch at school and I sometimes go out to a café near the school. The students finish school at 3:30 but I finish work at about 5:30 or sometimes 6. At the weekend, I never get up early. I always go out for breakfast with friends on Saturdays and I sometimes go to the gym in the afternoon. I like relaxing at the weekend.

1 Who does Julia live with?

_____

2 What job does she do?

_____

3 What time does she get up during the week?

_____

4 What does she have for breakfast?

_____

5 Where does she have lunch?

_____

6 What time does she finish work?

_____

7 Who does she have breakfast with on Saturdays?

_____

8 What does she do on Saturday afternoon?

_____

## REMEMBER THESE WORDS

**VERBS – ROUTINES AND FREE TIME**

| | |
|---|---|
| get up (late/early) | go to bed |
| have breakfast/lunch/dinner | go out with friends |
| go to work | have a party |
| start work | have a day off work |
| finish work | go on holiday |
| get home | |

**DAYS AND TIMES**

| | | | |
|---|---|---|---|
| Monday | Friday | three o'clock | midday |
| Tuesday | Saturday | two fifteen | midnight |
| Wednesday | Sunday | five thirty | |
| Thursday | | nine forty-five | |

**PREPOSITIONS WITH TIME EXPRESSIONS**

| | |
|---|---|
| on weekdays/Friday/Sunday morning | at two o'clock / three forty-five / the weekend |
| in the morning / the afternoon / the evening | every day/week/weekend/ month/year |

**OTHER**

| | | |
|---|---|---|
| busy | football match | celebrate |
| relax | doctor's appointment | tourists/tourism |
| (birthday) party | meeting | young |
| TV programme | exam | old |
| Tai Chi | (food/music) festival | |

## PRACTICE

**1** Complete the sentences with the verbs from the box.

get   gets up   go   go out   goes   finishes   has   have

1 He _____ to work by train every day.
2 She starts work at 9 and she _____ at 6:30.
3 I _____ a party for my birthday every year.
4 My parents _____ on holiday to Spain every year.
5 My brother _____ very late at the weekend.
6 They _____ with their friends every Friday evening.
7 My sister _____ lunch in a café every day.
8 I _____ home after 7 o'clock every evening.

**2** Write sentences about you using the verbs in exercise 1.

1 _____
2 _____
3 _____
4 _____
5 _____
6 _____
7 _____
8 _____

**3** Add the vowels (*a, e, i, o, u*) to complete the days of the week. Then write them in the correct order, starting with Monday.

1 S _ nd _ y
2 Th _ rsd _ y
3 S _ t _ rd _ y
4 T _ _ sd _ y
5 W _ dn _ sd _ y
6 Fr _ d _ y
7 M _ nd _ y

**4** Write the times.

1 4:00   *four o'clock*
2 3:15   _____
3 9:30   _____
4 11:45  _____
5 12 p.m.  _____
6 12 a.m.  _____

**5** Write the correct prepositions: *on, in, at* or *every*.

1 _____ Thursday
2 _____ four fifteen
3 _____ the afternoon
4 _____ week
5 _____ the evening
6 _____ Monday morning
7 _____ year
8 _____ the weekend

## STUDY 1

### can/can't

| + Positive | | | |
|---|---|---|---|
| subject | can/can't | verb | ... |
| I | **can** | swim | well. |
| You | **can** | play | the guitar. |
| He | **can't** (= cannot) | read | music. |
| She | **can't** (= cannot) | speak | French. |
| We | **can't** | talk | in class. |
| They | **can** | dance | well. |

## PRACTICE 1

**1 Put a line through the unnecessary words.**

*I ~~do~~ can't drive a car.*

1 You does can speak French.
2 He can't not play the piano.
3 She can to swim 100 metres.
4 I can't do cook Chinese food.
5 You can to ride a bike.
6 She does can't play chess.
7 I do can dance very well.
8 They can't not run fast.

**2 Write sentences about you using *can/can't* and the prompts.**

1 I / drive a car
2 I / play the guitar very well
3 I / ride a bike
4 I / cook Indian food
5 I / speak Chinese
6 I / sing very well
7 I / swim
8 I / play tennis

## STUDY 2

### Questions with *can*

| ? Questions | | | Short answers | |
|---|---|---|---|---|
| **Can** | you | cook? | Yes, I can. | No, I can't. |
| **Can** | he | play chess? | Yes, he can. | No, he can't. |
| **Can** | she | drive? | Yes, she can. | No, she can't. |
| **Can** | they | swim? | Yes, they can. | No, they can't. |

### REMEMBER!

We use *can/can't* in short answers (**NOT** *can/can't* + verb)
*Yes, she can.* **NOT** Yes, she can do. *No, he can't.* **NOT** No, he can't play.

## PRACTICE 2

**1 Put a line through the unnecessary words.**

1 Can he to speak English?
2 Can do you ride a bike?
3 Can she does cook well?
4 Can you to dance salsa?
5 Can your brother can run fast?
6 Can does she play tennis?
7 Can they to drive a car?
8 Can you do swim?

**2 Write questions and answers for each picture using *can / can't* and the words in brackets.**

1 (he/drive a car)
*Can he drive a car?*
*No, he can't.*

2 (she/sing)
_____
_____

3 (he/cook)
_____
_____

4 (they/dance salsa)
_____
_____

5 (she/swim)
_____
_____

6 (he/tennis)
_____
_____

7 (she/ride a bike)
_____
_____

8 (they/run fast)
_____
_____

## STUDY 3

### Review of questions

*Wh-* questions:
- with verb *be*: question word + *be* + subject
  *Who is* your teacher?
  *Why are* you late?
  *How many* people *are* in your class?
- with other verbs: question word + *do/does* OR *can* + subject + verb
  *What does* he *do* at work?
  *Where do* they *live*?
  *How many* languages *can* you *speak*?

*Yes/No* questions:
- with verb *be*: *be* + subject
  *Are you* from Italy?
  *Is she* a teacher?
  *Are they* at home today?
- with other verbs: *do/does* OR *can* + subject + verb
  *Do you* go to work by train?
  *Does she* live in a flat?
  *Can he* play the guitar?

## PRACTICE 3

**1 Choose the correct answers (a, b or c).**

1  Where _____ he live?
   **a** is    **b** does    **c** do
2  Where _____ he from?
   **a** is    **b** does    **c** do
3  _____ people are there in his family?
   **a** What    **b** Who    **c** How many
4  _____ his parents teachers?
   **a** Is    **b** Are    **c** Do
5  Does he _____ or study?
   **a** work    **b** job    **c** works
6  What _____ in his free time?
   **a** he does    **b** does he do    **c** he does do
7  Does he _____ sport?
   **a** plays    **b** like    **c** watches
8  _____ any foreign languages?
   **a** He can speak    **b** Can he speaks    **c** Can you speak

**2 Write questions from the sentences.**

1  He lives in Brazil. Where _____ ?
2  You can speak three languages. How many _____ ?
3  They are Italian. What nationality _____ ?
4  My teacher is in the classroom. Where _____ ?
5  She can play the piano. What musical instruments _____ ?
6  He goes to school by train. How _____ ?
7  They go to the cinema on Saturdays. What _____ ?
8  They are from Egypt. Where _____ ?

## REMEMBER THESE WORDS

**VERBS – THINGS YOU DO**

| | | |
|---|---|---|
| walk | swim | take photographs |
| run | dance | paint a picture |
| drive a car | sing | remember |
| ride a bike | play chess | forget |

**PARTS OF THE BODY**

| | | | |
|---|---|---|---|
| head | foot (feet) | nose | toe(s) |
| ear(s) | hair | mouth | |
| eye(s) | arm(s) | finger(s) | |
| hand(s) | leg(s) | thumb(s) | |

**OTHER**

| | | |
|---|---|---|
| (sing/cook ...) well | personal trainer | fit |
| (run/drive ...) fast | nanny | team games |
| skills | blow your nose | up/down the stairs |
| abilities | shake hands | be interested in |
| baby/babies | touch your toes | be good at |
| dance teacher | sporty | be good with |

## PRACTICE

**1 Complete the sentences with the verbs in the box. You can't use three of the verbs.**

take  remember  dance  drive  walk  paint  swim
play  ride  sing  forget

1  I _____ the guitar with friends every Saturday.
2  She can _____ over 100 metres in the swimming pool.
3  It's terrible! I never _____ my brother's birthday.
4  We always _____ a lot of photos on holiday.
5  Don't _____ to bring some money tomorrow!
6  I don't _____ my car in the town centre.
7  I _____ in the park with my dog every morning.
8  You can _____ your bike to work.

**2 Write sentences about you using the verbs in exercise 1.**

**3 Write parts of the body.**

1  DEHA = h _ _ _
2  MAR = a _ _
3  SENO = n _ _ _
4  OTHUM = m _ _ _ _

5  GENIRF = f _ _ _ _ _
6  MUBHT = t _ _ _ _
7  YEE = e _ _
8  TOFO = f _ _ _

**4 Choose the correct answers.**

1  I like playing *touch / team* games, e.g. basketball.
2  She can run very *fast / fit*.
3  She has only four *toes / fingers* on her foot.
4  It's terrible! I can't *remember / forget* phone numbers.
5  He can *drive / ride* a bike.
6  He isn't very good *at / with* playing the guitar.
7  My brother is very good *at / with* numbers.
8  I'm interested *in / with* history.

## STUDY 1

### Past simple of *be*: *was* and *were*

| I/he/she/it | |
|---|---|
| Positive | Negative |
| **I was** very happy. | **I wasn't** very happy. (= was not) |
| **She was** very good at swimming. | **He wasn't** a doctor. |
| **It was** an expensive car. | **It wasn't** a good book. |

| you/we/they | |
|---|---|
| Positive | Negative |
| **You were** at the cinema yesterday. | **You weren't** at the theatre. (= were not) |
| **We were** born in Argentina. | **We weren't** at school. |
| **They were** French. | **They weren't** Italian. |

### REMEMBER!

You can also use *was* and *were* with *there*:
*There was a large park.*
*There weren't any good restaurants.*

## PRACTICE 1

**1 Choose the correct answers.**

1 I *was* / *were* at the beach all day yesterday.
2 My sister and I *was* / *were* with my grandparents last week.
3 They *wasn't* / *weren't* at home yesterday.
4 You *was* / *were* at school on Tuesday.
5 Mario *was* / *were* born in Brazil.
6 My teacher *wasn't* / *weren't* in class on Monday.
7 The classroom *was* / *were* very hot yesterday.
8 You *wasn't* / *weren't* very happy as a child.

**2 Complete the sentences with *was*, *were*, *wasn't* or *weren't*.**

*My mother was from Argentina. (✓)*
*They weren't very happy about it. (✗)*

1 She _____ very good at playing tennis. (✓)
2 My cousins _____ at the party yesterday. (✗)
3 My teacher _____ at school today. (✗)
4 David and Nick _____ at the beach. (✓)
5 There _____ any tickets for the concert. (✗)
6 We _____ very good at dancing when we were young. (✓)
7 There _____ a café here before. (✓)
8 I _____ very happy when I was a child. (✗)

## STUDY 2

### Questions with *was* and *were*

| I/he/she/it | |
|---|---|
| Questions | Short answers |
| **Was I** late? | Yes, I **was**. |
| Who **was he**? | No, I **wasn't**. |
| **Was she** born in the USA? | Yes, he/she/it **was**. |
| What **was it**? | No, he/she/it **wasn't**. |

| you/we/they | |
|---|---|
| Questions | Short answers |
| Where **were you** born? | Yes, you/we/they **were**. |
| When **were we** in Italy? | No, you/we/they **weren't**. |
| **Were you** unhappy? | |
| Where **were they** from? | |

## PRACTICE 2

**1 Put a line through the unnecessary words.**

1 Where did was he born?
2 Were they be unhappy?
3 When were you was here before?
4 Was she did a teacher?
5 Why do were they late for class?
6 Where were you be yesterday?
7 Were you was on holiday last month?
8 Was that book does good?

**2a Complete the questions with *Was* or *Were*.**

1 _____ you at home yesterday?
2 _____ he happy at the weekend?
3 _____ they from Argentina?
4 _____ she interested in running?
5 _____ you good at playing the piano?
6 _____ it an interesting film?
7 _____ they at the cinema?
8 _____ he at the party on Saturday?

**b Write answers for the questions in exercise 2a, using the prompts.**

1 ✓ / I
2 ✗ / he
3 ✓ / they
4 ✓ / she
5 ✗ / I
6 ✓ / it
7 ✗ / they
8 ✗ / he

**3 Read the text and answer the questions.**

My grandfather, Gianni, was a singer. He was born in Rome in Italy in 1932. His parents weren't musicians. His father was an accountant and his mother was a maths teacher but they were happy about Gianni. He wasn't very good at maths but he was a very good singer.

1  What was Gianni's job?
_____

2  Where was Gianni born?
_____

3  Were his parents musicians?
_____

4  What was his father's job?
_____

5  What was his mother's job?
_____

6  Were they happy about Gianni's job?
_____

7  Was Gianni good at maths?
_____

8  Was he good at singing?
_____

## REMEMBER THESE WORDS

**MONTHS OF THE YEAR**

| | |
|---|---|
| January | July |
| February | August |
| March | September |
| April | October |
| May | November |
| June | December |

**ORDINAL NUMBERS AND DATES**

| | |
|---|---|
| the first of January | tenth |
| the second of April | eleventh |
| the third of December | twelfth |
| the fourth of August | thirteenth |
| fifth | fourteenth |
| sixth | fifteenth |
| seventh | twentieth |
| eighth | twenty-first |
| ninth | thirtieth |

**YEARS**

| | |
|---|---|
| 1900 = nineteen hundred | 2000 = two thousand |
| 1906 = nineteen oh six | 2005 = two thousand and five |
| 1945 = nineteen forty-five | 2010 = twenty ten |
| 1984 = nineteen eighty-four | 2012 = twenty twelve |

**OTHER**

| | |
|---|---|
| national holiday | noisy |
| President | clean |
| (vinyl) record | dirty |
| sporting event | naughty |
| quiet | yesterday |

**1a Add the vowels (a, e, i, o, u) to complete the months.**

1   S _ pt _ mb _ r
2   M _ y
3   J _ n _ _ ry
4   J _ ly
5   N _ v _ mb _ r
6   F _ br _ _ ry
7   M _ rch
8   J _ n _
9   _ pr _ l
10  D _ c _ mb _ r
11  _ _ g _ st
12  _ ct _ b _ r

**b Write the months in the correct order, starting with January.**

_____    _____
_____    _____
_____    _____
_____    _____
_____    _____
_____    _____

**2 Write the dates.**

20/05 – *the twentieth of May*
1  23/06 _____
2  19/03 _____
3  12/11 _____
4  17/05 _____
5  01/08 _____
6  31/12 _____
7  22/01 _____
8  03/03 _____

**3 Write the years.**

1963 – *nineteen sixty-three*
1  1988 _____
2  1990 _____
3  2007 _____
4  2014 _____
5  1979 _____
6  2000 _____
7  1909 _____
8  1999 _____

# 10 STUDY, PRACTICE & REMEMBER

## STUDY 1

### Past simple – regular verbs (positive)

| Most regular verbs: add -ed | Verbs ending in -e: add -d | Verbs ending in -y: change -y to -ied |
|---|---|---|
| start → started<br>work → worked<br>return → returned | live → lived<br>hate → hated | study → studied<br>marry → married |

**REMEMBER!**

The Past simple is the **same** for *I, you, he, she, it, we* and *they*.

**REMEMBER!**

We sometimes use these words and phrases with the Past simple:

*yesterday*

*(two years) ago*

*last night/week/month/year*

*I started my homework **yesterday**.*

*She lived in Madrid **five years ago**.*

*They studied English **last year**.*

## PRACTICE 1

**1 Choose the correct answers.**

1 I **work / worked** for a big company now.
2 She **lives / lived** in London three years ago.
3 They **return / returned** home yesterday.
4 He **studies / studied** Russian now.
5 We **start / started** dance classes two days ago.
6 He **marries / married** his girlfriend last weekend.
7 We **live / lived** in a flat now.
8 I **hate / hated** vegetables when I was a child.

**2 Complete the sentences with the Past simple forms of the verbs in brackets.**

I *started* (start) a business with my friend Jack.
1 My parents _____ (work) in a hospital.
2 He _____ (design) the new train station.
3 She _____ (die) at the age of 79.
4 I _____ (move) to the USA when I was three.
5 They _____ (study) engineering at university.
6 Martina _____ (live) in Russia for three years.
7 He _____ (marry) a woman from Argentina.
8 They _____ (create) an online company last year.

## STUDY 2

### Past simple – regular verbs (negative)

For the Past simple negative form: *did + not + verb*

*I studied English. I **didn't study** English.*

*He worked long hours. He **didn't work** long hours.*

*They stayed in a hotel. They **didn't stay** in a hotel.*

**REMEMBER!**

| Present simple | Past simple |
|---|---|
| *I **don't like** football.* | *I **didn't like** football.* |
| *He **doesn't live** in London.* | *He **didn't live** in London.* |
| *She **doesn't study** maths.* | *She **didn't study** maths.* |
| *They **don't start** work.* | *They **didn't start** work.* |

## PRACTICE 2

**1 Six of the sentences have a missing word. Write the missing word in the correct place. Tick the two correct sentences.**

1 She not like playing computer games.
2 My parents not live in the city centre.
3 I did not go to the beach last weekend.
4 My teacher not come to class today.
5 We did not in a hotel last year.
6 My sister didn't study at university.
7 You not start work early yesterday.
8 He not pass his driving test.

**2 Choose the correct answers.**

1 He **doesn't / didn't** like computer games now.
2 They **don't / didn't** live in Paris last year.
3 I **don't / didn't** stay in a hotel last week.
4 They **don't / didn't** study at university now.
5 She **doesn't / didn't** work for a big company two years ago.
6 We **don't / didn't** return to work last week.
7 He **doesn't / didn't** live in a small flat now.
8 I **don't / didn't** start my course last Monday.

**3 Rewrite the sentences in exercise 2 of Practice 1 using the negative forms of the verbs in the Past simple.**

*I didn't start a business with my friend Jack.*

1 _____
2 _____
3 _____
4 _____
5 _____
6 _____
7 _____
8 _____

## STUDY 3

### Past simple – irregular verbs (positive and negative)

- Many common verbs have irregular past forms:
  go → *went*
  have → *had*
  write → *wrote*
  make → *made*

- For the Past simple negative form: *did + not +* verb

  | | |
  |---|---|
  | They **went** to the beach. | They **didn't go** to the beach. |
  | He **had** three dogs. | He **didn't have** three dogs. |
  | I **bought** a house last year. | I **didn't buy** a house last year. |
  | We **left** work at 5.30. | We **didn't leave** work at 5.30. |
  | They **got** married. | They **didn't get** married. |

#### REMEMBER!

When we form the negative with the Past simple, we use *didn't +* verb (**NOT** *didn't +* Past simple)

*I **didn't go** to the beach yesterday.* **NOT** *I didn't went to the beach yesterday.*

*They **didn't buy** a new car.* **NOT** *They didn't bought a new car.*

## PRACTICE 3

**1a Write the Past simple forms of the verbs.**

1 buy: _____
2 go: _____
3 get: _____
4 have: _____
5 leave: _____
6 make: _____
7 meet: _____
8 win: _____

**b Complete the sentences with the Past simple forms from exercise 1a.**

1 They _____ to Spain on holiday last year.
2 My brother _____ a new car last week.
3 She _____ her husband at work.
4 I _____ a cake for my sister's birthday.
5 They _____ married in Thailand.
6 He _____ the house at 7.30 this morning.
7 My friend _____ a prize in a singing competition.
8 They _____ a daughter called Oriana in 2011.

**2 Rewrite the sentences in the negative form.**

1 We went to the beach last week.
2 He bought a new car last weekend.
3 They got married two months ago.
4 I wrote an essay yesterday.
5 They had a great holiday last month.
6 She left work early last Friday.
7 We had three cats when I was a child.
8 I went to the cinema yesterday.

## REMEMBER THESE WORDS

**VERBS – LIFE EVENTS**

| | |
|---|---|
| leave (primary/secondary) school | meet your partner/someone |
| go to university | special |
| leave university | get married |
| pass your driving test | buy a house or flat |
| get your first job | have children |
| start a business | |

**CREATIVE JOBS**

| | |
|---|---|
| artist | architect |
| musician | inventor |
| singer | film director |
| dancer | fashion designer |
| writer | |

**OTHER**

| | |
|---|---|
| computer scientist | search engine |
| prize | plane |
| award | bridge |
| TV show | jewellery |

## PRACTICE

**1 Complete the sentences with the verbs in the box.**

| buy | get | go | have | leave (x2) | meet | pass |
|---|---|---|---|---|---|---|

Most people in the UK:

1 _____ primary school when they are 11.
2 _____ to university when they are 18.
3 _____ their husband or wife at work.
4 _____ married when they are over 25.
5 _____ children when they are over 25.
6 _____ their driving test when they are 18 or 19.
7 _____ a house when they are over 30.
8 _____ university when they are 21.

**2 Write sentences about your own country using the ideas in exercise 1.**

Most people in my country:

1 _____  5 _____
2 _____  6 _____
3 _____  7 _____
4 _____  8 _____

**3 Add vowels (*a, e, i, o* and *u*) to complete the words.**

1 d _ nc _ r
2 _ rt _ st
3 _ nv _ nt _ r
4 _ rch _ t _ ct
5 wr _ t _ r
6 s _ ng _ r
7 f _ lm d _ r _ ct _ r
8 m _ s _ c _ _ n
9 f _ sh _ _ n d _ s _ gn _ r

## STUDY 1

### Past simple: *Yes/No* questions

| Yes/No questions | | | |
|---|---|---|---|
| **Did** | **subject** | **verb** | |
| Did | you | go | on holiday? |
| Did | he | visit | his cousins? |
| Did | they | buy | a return ticket? |
| Did | she | make | a cake? |
| **Short answers** | | | |
| Yes, I did. | NOT ~~Yes, I went.~~ | | |
| No, I didn't. | NOT ~~No, I didn't go.~~ | | |

**REMEMBER!**

The Past simple question form is the same for *I, you, he, she, it, we* and *they*.

**REMEMBER!**

We don't use *did* in questions with *was* and *were*.
*Was* the weather good?
*Were* you at home yesterday?

## PRACTICE 1

**1 Put a line through the unnecessary words.**

1 **A:** Did you ~~bought~~ buy some new jeans?
   **B:** Yes, I did ~~buy~~.
2 **A:** Did she ~~did~~ go to work yesterday?
   **B:** No, she didn't go.
3 **A:** Did ~~play~~ they play football last weekend?
   **B:** No, they didn't ~~played~~.
4 **A:** Did you ~~saw~~ see Amelia yesterday.
   **B:** Yes, I did ~~saw~~.

**2 Complete the questions and answers using the prompts.**

1 **A:** _____ (you/go) by train?
   **B:** Yes, I _____ .
2 **A:** _____ (they/play) tennis yesterday?
   **B:** No, they _____ .
3 **A:** _____ (he/cook) dinner yesterday?
   **B:** Yes, he _____ .
4 **A:** _____ (she/study) French at university?
   **B:** No, she _____ .
5 **A:** _____ (you/see) the football match?
   **B:** Yes, I _____ .
6 **A:** _____ (he/pass) his driving test?
   **B:** No, he _____ .
7 **A:** _____ (she/get) the job?
   **B:** Yes, she _____ .
8 **A:** _____ (they/enjoy) the holiday?
   **B:** No, they _____ .

## STUDY 2

### Past simple: *Wh-* questions

| Wh- questions | | | | |
|---|---|---|---|---|
| **Question word** | **did** | **subject** | **verb** | |
| What | did | you | do | last weekend? |
| When | did | she | leave | work? |
| Who | did | they | go | on holiday with? |
| Why | did | he | phone | you? |

**REMEMBER!**

The Past simple question form is the same for *I, you, he, she, it, we* and *they*.

**REMEMBER!**

We don't use *did* in questions with *was* and *were*.
*What **was** the weather like?*
*How many people **were** in the class?*

## PRACTICE 2

**1 Write the words in the correct order to make questions.**

1 did / Where / you / yesterday / go?
2 the weather / was / What / like?
3 you / Who / live / last year / with / did?
4 did / Why / they / those books / buy?
5 people / How many / at the concert / were?
6 last weekend / do / What / he / did?
7 this morning / did / you / get up / When?
8 born / Where / you / were?

**2 Complete the questions.**

1 **A:** Where _____ on holiday?
   **B:** She went to Australia.
2 **A:** When _____ ?
   **B:** They went in July.
3 **A:** Who _____ with?
   **B:** He travelled with his sister.
4 **A:** What _____ at university?
   **B:** I studied engineering.
5 **A:** How many countries _____ last year?
   **B:** She visited five countries.
6 **A:** When _____ that car?
   **B:** He bought it last week.
7 **A:** Who _____ with yesterday?
   **B:** I played tennis with Mario.
8 **A:** When _____ that new film?
   **B:** She saw it last weekend.

**3 Look at the pictures and write the answers.**

Where did he go last weekend?

*He went skiing.*

1 Where did she go last weekend?

_____
_____

2 Who did you go to the cinema with?

_____
_____

3 What was the weather like last weekend?

_____
_____

4 When did the film start?

_____
_____

5 What did you make?

_____
_____

6 What did you do on Saturday?

_____
_____

7 What time did you get up this morning?

_____
_____

8 How many people were in the classroom?

_____
_____

## REMEMBER THESE WORDS

**TRANSPORT AND TRAVEL**

| | | |
|---|---|---|
| go by bus/train/plane/... | buy a return (ticket) | be late |
| go on a journey | buy a travel card | be early |
| buy a single (ticket) | be on time | |

**TIME EXPRESSIONS**

| | | |
|---|---|---|
| in August/2013 | last week/month/year | first |
| a year/two months/ | yesterday (morning/ | then |
| three weeks ago | afternoon/evening) | after that |
| | | in the end |

**HOLIDAY ACTIVITIES**

| | | |
|---|---|---|
| eat out | go on a boat trip | go walking |
| visit museums | go sightseeing | go skiing |
| go shopping | go to the beach | |

**OTHER**

| | | |
|---|---|---|
| dangerous | airport | raise money (for charity) |
| to cross / to go across | tunnel | a bike ride / to ride |
| flight | passenger | a bike |

## PRACTICE

**1 Add vowels (*a*, *e*, *i*, *o* and *u*) to complete the words.**

1 j _ _ rn _ y
2 tr _ v _ l c _ rd
3 r _ t _ rn t _ ck _ t
4 y _ st _ rd _ y
5 m _ s _ _ m
6 s _ ghts _ _ _ ng
7 b _ _ t tr _ p
8 _ _ rp _ rt

**2 Complete the sentences with the words in the box. You do not need three of the words.**

sightseeing   single   trip   skiing   time   early   out
return   travel card   late   visited

1 I went _____ in the mountains in Italy last winter.
2 When I go on holiday, I like eating _____ in local restaurants.
3 She bought a _____ ticket from Paris to Milan and back.
4 They went on a boat _____ around the Greek islands.
5 Her plane was on _____ – it arrived at exactly 3 p.m.
6 I love going _____ when I visit a new city.
7 We _____ three museums when we went to London.
8 My train was _____ so I missed the film.

**3 Choose the correct answers.**

1 She moved to New Zealand *on* / *in* 2012.
2 I took my exam three days *ago* / *then*.
3 In the *final* / *end*, we got home very late.
4 The course started *last* / *yesterday* week.
5 *Then* / *That*, they went on a boat trip.
6 He bought the tickets *last* / *yesterday* morning.
7 *First* / *Final*, he went by taxi to the airport.
8 *Later* / *After* that, I played football with some friends.

## STUDY 1

### *want* and *want to*

| *want* + noun | I **want** a mobile phone.<br>She **doesn't want** any jewellery.<br>**Do** you **want** some new shoes? |
|---|---|
| *want to* + verb | We **want to** go to the beach.<br>He **doesn't want to** watch TV.<br>**Does** she **want to** go swimming? |

## PRACTICE 1

**1 Six of the sentences have a missing word. Write the missing words in the correct place. Tick the two correct sentences.**

1 I want go to the cinema.
2 She wants new computer for her birthday.
3 What you want to do on Saturday?
4 Does he want to go to university?
5 They want travel around the world.
6 Where does she want go for her holiday?
7 I don't want a cup of tea at the moment.
8 He doesn't want fail his exam.

**2 Complete the sentences with *want to/want a*, *don't/doesn't want(s) to* or *don't/doesn't want(s) a*.**

1 I _____ go to Mexico on holiday. (✔)
2 He _____ dog for his birthday. (✔)
3 They _____ see that film. (✗)
4 She _____ go swimming today. (✗)
5 They _____ house near the beach. (✔)
6 I _____ new car. (✗)
7 You _____ buy some jeans. (✔)
8 He _____ beach holiday this year. (✗)

**3 Read the answers and write the questions.**

1 A: What _____
   B: She wants to go on holiday.
2 A: What _____
   B: He wants a new car.
3 A: Where _____
   B: They want to go to Italy.
4 A: Who _____
   B: She wants to go with her sister.
5 A: What _____
   B: They want to have a party.
6 A: What _____
   B: I want a cup of tea.
7 A: What _____
   B: They want to play football.
8 A: Where _____
   B: He wants to go to the cinema.

## STUDY 2

### *going to*

| be + (not) *going to* + verb | |
|---|---|
| Positive | I'm **going to meet** some friends tomorrow.<br>She's **going to play** tennis this afternoon.<br>We're **going to see** a film tonight.<br>They're **going to get** married next month. |
| Negative | I'm **not going to come** to class tomorrow.<br>He's **not going to play** football next weekend. |
| Questions | What **are** you **going to do** this evening?<br>**Is** she **going to make** a cake? |

### REMEMBER!

We sometimes use these words and phrases with *going to*:
*tonight*
*tomorrow*
*this afternoon/evening*
*next week/weekend/month/year*

## PRACTICE 2

**1 Put a line through the unnecessary words.**

1 I'm be going to buy a new bike.
2 Is she is going to phone her boss?
3 They're not to going to come skiing with us.
4 Where do are you going to go this weekend?
5 We're going go to go to a party on Saturday.
6 Are you are going to get up early tomorrow?
7 She's not be going to study languages.
8 What are going you going to do after work?

**2 Write sentences using *going to* and the words given.**

1 I / visit my parents tomorrow.
2 She / take her driving test next week.
3 We / not / buy a new car this year.
4 I / not / get up early tomorrow morning.
5 They / have a party next weekend.
6 He / not / come shopping with us on Saturday.
7 I / have lunch with Julia tomorrow.
8 You / not / finish that book this afternoon.

**3 Look at the pictures and answer the questions.**

1  Is she going to get a cat?
_____

2  Are they going to watch TV?
_____

3  What are they going to do?
_____

4  Is he going to play football?
_____

5  Are they going to get on the bus?
_____

6  Where are they going to go?
_____

7  Is she going to buy the jacket?
_____

8  What is he going to do?
_____

## REMEMBER THESE WORDS

**WANTS – VERB PHRASES**

get a cat

go diving

see the Northern Lights

travel round the world

join a singing group

start a football team

do a course in jewellery making

take part in a TV quiz show

meet a famous film star

perform on stage

**THINGS YOU CAN BUY**

clothes

jewellery

accessories

technology

a T-shirt

a jacket

jeans

earrings

a necklace

a bracelet

an umbrella

a handbag

a scarf

---

**DESCRIBING OBJECTS: COLOURS AND SIZES**

red

orange

yellow

green

blue

purple

brown

white

black

grey

small

medium

large

extra-large

**OTHER**

fun

boring

frightening

exciting

sociable

creative

carry

buy online

## PRACTICE

**1 Complete the sentences with the verbs from the box.**

do   get   go   join   meet   perform   take part   travel

1  I'm going to _____ a cat soon.
2  When I go on holiday, I'm going to _____ diving.
3  I'm going to _____ a singing group in my area.
4  I really want to _____ in a TV quiz show.
5  He wants to _____ on stage with his band.
6  She's going to _____ a course in making clothes.
7  She wants to _____ Brad Pitt – her favourite film star.
8  They're going to _____ round the world on a motorbike.

**2 Add vowels (a, e, i, o and u) to complete the words.**

1  bl _ ck
2  br _ wn
3  gr _ y
4  p _ rpl _
5  gr _ _ n
6  bl _ _
7  r _ d
8  _ r _ ng _
9  y _ ll _ w
10  wh _ t _

**3 Put the words in the box into the correct category.**

yellow   a necklace   medium   an umbrella   a bracelet
extra-large   a scarf   purple   a jacket   jeans

1  **colours:** _____

2  **sizes:** _____

3  **jewellery:** _____

4  **accessories:** _____

5  **clothes:** _____

# Audio script

## UNIT 1 RECORDING 2

1 A: Hi, I'm Kate.
   B: Hello, Kate. My name's James. Nice to meet you.
2 A: Hello, my name's Tom.
   B: Hi, Tom. I'm Juliet. Nice to meet you.
3 A: Hello, my name's Steve.
   B: Hello, Steve. My name's Kara. Nice to meet you.

## UNIT 1 RECORDING 4

1 Hello, I'm Daniel.
2 Are you Tom?
3 Hi. Are you Sarah?
4 I'm Anton.
5 Hello, my name's Kate.
6 What's your name?
7 My name's Masumi.
8 Hi. What's your name?

## UNIT 1 RECORDING 5

1 A: Hello, my name's Harry.
   B: Hi, Harry. I'm Sandra. Nice to meet you.
2 A: Are you Michael?
   B: Yes, that's right.
3 A: What's your name?
   B: My name's Simon Dodds.
4 A: Hi, I'm Julia.
   B: Hello, Julia. My name's Jenny.
5 A: Are you Kim Watson?
   B: No, I'm Kim Watts.
6 A: What's your name?
   B: My name's Mike.

## UNIT 1 RECORDING 8

1 A: What's your job?
   B: I'm a teacher.
2 A: Are you an engineer?
   B: No, I'm an architect.
3 A: Are you a shop assistant?
   B: Yes, that's right.
4 A: Are you a student?
   B: No, I'm an accountant.

## UNIT 2 RECORDING 3

A: Where are you from?
B: I'm from Australia. And you?
A: I'm from Italy.
B: Really? Are you from Rome?
A: No, I'm not. I'm from Milan.

## UNIT 2 RECORDING 4

1 A: Is Daniel Day Lewis a director?
   B: No, he isn't. He's an actor.
2 A: Is he from England?
   B: Yes, he is.
3 A: Is London in the USA?
   B: No, it isn't. It's in England.
4 A: Is Rebecca Miller from England?
   B: No, she isn't. She's from the USA.
5 A: Where's Connecticut?
   B: It's in the USA.

## UNIT 2 RECORDING 5

1 A: Is your teacher from Australia?
   B: No, she isn't.
2 A: Where's Nawal El Saadawi from?
   B: She's from Egypt.

3 A: Is Barack Obama from the USA?
   B: Yes, he is.
4 A: Is your best friend from Russia?
   B: No, he isn't.
5 A: Where's Dilma Rousseff from?
   B: I don't know.

## UNIT 2 RECORDING 9

1 A: What's her name?
   B: Her name's Marianna.
2 A: Where's he from?
   B: He's from Egypt. He's Egyptian.
3 A: Is his name Antonio?
   B: No, it isn't. His name's Anton.
4 A: Where's she from?
   B: She's from Japan. She's Japanese.
5 A: What's his job?
   B: He's a teacher.
6 A: Where's she from?
   B: She's from Spain. She's Spanish.

## UNIT 2 RECORDING 13

twenty
twenty-one
twenty-two
twenty-three
twenty-four
twenty-five
twenty-six
twenty-seven
twenty-eight
twenty-nine

## UNIT 3 RECORDING 3

1 What's the name of that shop?
2 These people are Spanish.
3 Who are those children?
4 Look at this place!
5 Is that your bus?
6 These students are my friends.
7 Who are those women?
8 This country is beautiful!

## UNIT 3 RECORDING 4

A A: Who's that man?
   B: He's my teacher.
B A: Alex, this is James.
   B: Hello, James.
C A: Where are those people from?
   B: They're from Italy.
D A: These two books, please.
   B: Ten pounds, please.

## UNIT 3 RECORDING 6

1 The people are friendly.
2 The hotel is cheap.
3 We are happy.
4 The holiday is fantastic.

## UNIT 3 RECORDING 8

My name's Joana and I'm from Kraków in Poland. My friends Giulia and Massimo are also students. They aren't from Poland – they are from Italy. We are in Boston now – we are students at the university.

Our flat is very expensive, but the shops aren't expensive. The people are very friendly – Boston is a fantastic city!

## UNIT 3 RECORDING 9

Sumiko and I are from Tokyo in Japan and we are engineers. We aren't in Japan now – we are in Sydney in Australia for a conference. Alex and Kim are also engineers. They aren't from Japan – they are from Brazil. Sydney is a great city and the conference is fantastic. But the restaurant in the hotel isn't good – the food is awful and the waiters are unfriendly.

## UNIT 3 RECORDING 11

1 Drink: tea, coffee, milk, water
2 Meat and fish: chicken
3 Fruit: apples
4 Vegetables: potatoes
5 Other food: bread, rice, pasta, eggs, cheese

## UNIT 4 RECORDING 3

1 The car park is near the train station.
2 The supermarket is on the right of the bank.
3 The café isn't in the square.
4 The bus stop is near the café.
5 The park is near the train station.
6 The supermarket is in Station Road.
7 The hotel is on the right of the car park.
8 The shopping centre is on the left of the cinema.

## UNIT 4 RECORDING 4

1 There are three apples on the table.
2 There's a bottle of water in my bag.
3 There's an Italian restaurant near here.
4 There are two people in the car.
5 There's a bank next to the supermarket.
6 There are five children in the cinema.

## UNIT 4 RECORDING 6

1 There is a beautiful square in the city centre.
2 There are some taxis near the train station.
3 Is there a cinema near here?
4 Are there any buses to the shopping centre?
5 There aren't any cheap hotels in the city centre.
6 There are a lot of big shops in this area.
7 There isn't a train station in my town.
8 Are there any supermarkets near here?

## UNIT 4 RECORDING 7

A a mountain
B an island
C a lake
D the sea
E a river
F a rainforest
G a hill
H a beach

## UNIT 4 RECORDING 8

1 The Mediterranean is a famous sea.
2 There are about **1,400** islands in Greece.
3 There are over three million lakes in Canada.
4 The Nile is a river. It's about **6,650** kilometres long.
5 There are about **40,000** different plants in the Amazon rainforest.
6 Mount Fuji is a mountain in Japan. It's **3,776** metres high.
7 Copacabana is a famous beach in Brazil.
8 There are seven hills in the city of Rome.

## UNIT 5 RECORDING 2

1 Dylan is Sonia's brother.
2 Tom is Anna's husband.
3 Sonia and Laura are Dylan's sisters.
4 Sonia's mother's name is Anna.
5 Alice is Tony's wife.

6 Helena is Sonia's grandmother.
7 Tom's father's name is George.
8 Tony and Alice are Sonia's grandparents.

## UNIT 5 RECORDING 3

1 Ellie and her friends live in a flat.
2 David and Sophie don't live in London now.
3 David and Sophie teach English to university students.
4 David and Sophie work at Shanghai University.
5 Harry and Holly speak Chinese with their friends.
6 Harry and Holly don't go to school in England.
7 Ellie and her friends study at London University.
8 David and Sophie don't have three children.

## UNIT 5 RECORDING 4

1 go to school, go home for lunch, go to work by bus
2 have children, have two brothers, have a car
3 live in a flat, live in a house, live with your family
4 study medicine, study at university, study languages
5 work in an office, work for a big company, work long hours

## UNIT 5 RECORDING 6

1 Where do you live?
2 Do you live in the town centre?
3 Do you live in a house or a flat?
4 Who do you live with?
5 Do you have any children?
6 Do you work or study near your home?
7 Do you go to work or school by car?
8 Do you study English at school?

## UNIT 5 RECORDING 9

My name is Talya and I'm twenty-six. I'm from Turkey. My parents are from Marmaris – a small town by the sea but now we live in Istanbul. It's a big city but the people are very friendly.

I live with my family in a flat near the city centre. I'm an artist and a photographer. I work for a magazine company – I take photos for the magazine. I also paint pictures and sell them in an art gallery. It's difficult to make money ... but I love my job.

I live with my parents and my brother. My brother's name is Emre and he's nineteen. He's a student at the university. My father's name is Ali and my mother's name is Mira. They're teachers – they work in a secondary school.

## UNIT 6 RECORDING 2

**Tom**

My friend Tom is thirteen years old and he lives with his family here in Melbourne. I see Tom at school, but he doesn't go out with me or his other friends a lot because he's very busy. He cooks dinner for his family every day! He's a very good cook – in fact, he's the winner of a junior cooking competition here in Australia. He reads books a lot – but only books about food and cooking!

**Annie**

Today is my grandmother's birthday! Her name's Annie and she's seventy years old today. I think she's an amazing person because she's a very busy and active woman. She doesn't go to the gym because it's boring. But she plays tennis every day with her friends and she usually wins! She also uses the computer a lot – she likes talking to friends on it.

## UNIT 6 RECORDING 4

1 My mother cooks dinner every day.
2 He plays football with his friends.
3 Diana doesn't use the laptop every day.
4 My friends go to the cinema a lot.
5 She watches TV every day.
6 My parents don't read magazines.
7 Miguel uses a computer at work.
8 He has a lot of friends.

# Audio script

## UNIT 7 RECORDING 2

A eleven o'clock
B six thirty
C one fifteen
D two forty-five
E eight fifteen
F twelve forty-five
G seven o'clock
H nine thirty

## UNIT 7 RECORDING 4

1 I never start work at 7.00 a.m.
2 I usually feel tired in the morning.
3 I don't usually have breakfast.
4 I sometimes go to work by train.
5 I always have lunch in a restaurant.
6 I usually go to bed late.
7 I never work in the evening.
8 I don't usually get up early.

## UNIT 7 RECORDING 8

A: The Kawhia Kai Festival is one of my favourite days of the year.
B: Kawhia Kai Festival – what's that?
A: Well, it's a local food festival in my town.
B: What does the festival celebrate?
A: We celebrate all the local food which we get in the area ... from the land, and from the sea.
B: The local food?
A: Yes, the name of the festival is Kawhia Kai. Kawhia is the name of my town – it's a small town by the sea and kai is the local word for 'food'. We have a lot of delicious fish and meat.
B: When is the festival?
A: It's on the sixth of February every year.
B: The sixth of February? Why does it happen on that day? Is it a special day?
A: Yes, it's Waitangi Day or New Zealand Day. We celebrate our country's independence on that day, and we also celebrate the food that the country gives us ... the country, the land, the sea, the food ... you know ... all of that.
B: Mmm ... so, where does the festival take place?
A: There are celebrations all around the town and on the beach. There's a lot of food to eat and also other things to do like listening to music and other entertainment for the visitors.
B: And who are the visitors? Is it just for local people ... or are there tourists, too?
A: There are local people and tourists.
B: And is it a big festival? I mean, how many people are there?
A: A lot of people go to the festival. I think there are about 10,000 people. It's great ... it's a really good festival ... I love it!

## UNIT 7 RECORDING 9

1 A: What is your favourite special day or festival?
   B: It's the Cambridge Music Festival.
2 A: What do people do?
   B: People listen to live music – singers and musicians.
3 A: When is the festival?
   B: It's in the summer ... in July.
4 A: Where does it take place?
   B: It's in a park in Cambridge.
5 A: How many people are there?
   B: I think there are usually about 10,000 people.
6 A: Who do you go with?
   B: I always go with six friends.
7 A: Why do you go?
   B: Because we all love music ... and it's a really fun festival.

## UNIT 7 RECORDING 11

1 on Friday
  on weekdays
  on Sunday morning
2 in the evening
  in the morning
  in the afternoon
3 at two o'clock
  at the weekend
  at three forty-five
4 every week
  every day
  every weekend

## UNIT 8 RECORDING 1

1 I take a lot of photographs when I go on holiday.
2 I walk to work every day because I don't like going by bus.
3 I love swimming in the sea when I go on holiday.
4 I usually play chess with my grandfather on Sunday afternoons.
5 I like dancing when I go to a party with my friends.
6 I run in the park at the weekend because I want to keep fit.
7 I always paint a picture of the beach when I go on holiday.
8 I never drive my car to the town centre because it's very busy.
9 I ride a bike to work in the summer but not in the winter.
10 I like listening to music in the car and singing the songs.

## UNIT 8 RECORDING 2

1 He can't play chess.
2 They can swim 25 metres.
3 She can't remember all her friends' birthdays.
4 He can't play the piano.
5 He can cook well.
6 They can't drive.
7 You can speak a foreign language.
8 I can't run fast.
9 She can read music.
10 They can't dance very well.

## UNIT 8 RECORDING 6

In India, you eat with your hands – but you can only use your right hand.
In Thailand, you can't put your feet on a chair – it isn't polite.
In Japan, you can't blow your nose in public – it isn't polite.
In Dubai, you shake hands when you meet someone – but you can only use your right hand.
In the USA, when you talk to someone, you can show interest by looking at his or her eyes.
In Britain, you can say 'OK' or 'I like it' by holding your thumb up.
In Bulgaria, you can say 'yes' by moving your head from side to side, and you can say 'no' by moving your head up and down.

## UNIT 8 RECORDING 8

1 What sports do you like doing?
2 Can you run ten kilometres?
3 Do you walk to school or work every day?
4 Can you stand on your hands?
5 How many days a week do you do exercise?
6 Do you usually run up the stairs?

## UNIT 9 RECORDING 3

A thirteenth
B fifteenth
C seventeenth
D nineteenth
E twentieth
F twenty-second
G thirtieth
H thirty-first

## UNIT 9 RECORDING 7

A  Ronald Reagan was President of the USA. He was seventy-five years old.

B  The number one film of the year was *Top Gun*, with American film star Tom Cruise. Other popular films in that year were *Crocodile Dundee*, with Australian actor Paul Hogan, and *Karate Kid*, with Italian-American actor Ralph Macchio.

C  Germany wasn't a single country. There were two countries called 'Germany' – East and West. Bonn was the capital of West Germany and East Berlin was the capital of East Germany.

D  The FIFA World Cup was in Mexico – and the winners were Argentina. Diego Maradona was the captain of the winning team.

E  There weren't any DVDs, laptops or iPads. Vinyl records were still popular.

F  There were twelve countries in the European Union. Poland and Hungary weren't members of the European Union.

## UNIT 9 RECORDING 11

1  Rafael Nadal was born in Manacor, Spain in **1986**.
2  Daniel Craig was born in Chester, UK in **1968**.
3  Harper Beckham, David and Victoria's daughter, was born in Los Angeles, USA in **2011**.
4  Priyanka Chopra was born in Jamshedpur, India in **1982**.
5  Nelson Mandela was born in Mvezo, South Africa in **1918**.
6  Shakira was born in Barranquilla, Colombia in **1977**.

## UNIT 9 RECORDING 12

M = Marta   J = Jack

M:  Jack ... you're a noisy person now. When you were a child, were you quiet or noisy?

J:  Oh! I was noisy! Yes, I was a noisy child ... always talking and playing with my friends ... and my brother ... I was always with my brother.

M:  Your brother?

J:  Yes.

M:  Who was your favourite person in your family?

J:  Hmm ... that's a difficult question ... umm ... My brother and I were very good friends, but I think my favourite person was my grandfather ... yes, he was my favourite.

M:  And who was your best friend when you were a child?

J:  Uh ... my best friend was a boy called Tim ... and we were very good friends. We were in the same class at school.

M:  What was your favourite subject at school?

J:  Er ... I can't remember ... erm ... I was happy at school. I was interested in lots of things. I think my favourite subject was maths.

M:  And, were you good at sport?

J:  No, I wasn't! I wasn't good at sport at all but I was always in the park with my bike! My bike was my favourite thing. It was great!

## UNIT 10 RECORDING 1

Larry Page was born in the USA in 1973. As a child, he loved computers and he studied computer science at university. In 1998, he created the search engine company Google. The company was very successful and he is now a multi-millionaire.

Henri Matisse was born in France in 1869. He started painting when he was 20 and he worked with many other painters including Picasso. He married Amélie Noellie Parayre in 1898 and lived most of his life in France. He died in France in 1954.

American writer Toni Morrison was born in 1931. As a child she liked reading books. Her favourite writers were Jane Austen and Leo Tolstoy. She moved to New York in 1964 and started writing. In 1988, she received a prize for her book, *Beloved*.

British dancer Darcey Bussell was born in London in 1969, but she lived in Australia during her early childhood. She worked as the principal dancer at the Royal Ballet in London when she was only twenty. In 2009, she started work on a TV dance show.

## UNIT 10 RECORDING 2

died
liked
started
received
studied
created
married
worked

## UNIT 10 RECORDING 3

Leonardo da Vinci was an artist, a scientist and a designer. He was born in the small town of Vinci in Italy in 1452. As a child, he studied painting in the city of Florence. In 1482, when he was thirty, he moved to Milan. He lived and worked there for many years.

Da Vinci was famous as a great artist. He painted *The Last Supper* in 1498 and *La Gioconda* (the *Mona Lisa*) in 1503. He was also a great designer. He designed early planes and bridges.

In 1516, near the end of his life, he moved to France. He died in France in 1519, aged 67.

## UNIT 10 RECORDING 4

become – became
buy – bought
get – got
go – went
have – had
leave – left
make – made
meet – met
sell – sold
win – won

## UNIT 10 RECORDING 6

1  I left my job in 2010.
2  She went to university to study business.
3  He sold his business for a lot of money.
4  They bought a flat in the town centre.
5  I met my husband last year.
6  He won a prize for his music.
7  They got married on a beach.
8  She became an actor in 1999.
9  They had three children – two sons and a daughter.
10  He made a lot of money from his business.

## UNIT 10 RECORDING 7

1  I didn't leave my job in 2010.
2  She didn't go to university to study business.
3  He didn't sell his business for a lot of money.
4  They didn't buy a flat in the town centre.
5  I didn't meet my husband last year.
6  He didn't win a prize for his music.
7  They didn't get married on a beach.
8  She didn't become an actor in 1999.
9  They didn't have three children – two sons and a daughter.
10  He didn't make a lot of money from his business.

## UNIT 11 RECORDING 3

1  Did you buy a single ticket?
2  Did you have a good journey?
3  Were you tired?
4  Did you buy a travel card?
5  Were you on time?

# Audio script

## UNIT 11 RECORDING 5

M = Mark    J = Juliet
a  M: Why did you go?
   J:  It was for charity.
b  M: When did you go?
   J:  I went in July last year.
c  M: Where did you go?
   J:  I went to the USA.
d  M: Who did you go with?
   J:  I went with a group of twenty-two people.
e  M: How did you feel during the ride?
   J:  I often felt really tired!
f  M: How much money did you raise?
   J:  I raised about £3,000.
g  M: How long were you there for?
   J:  I was there for about two weeks in total.
h  M: What was the weather like?
   J:  It was very, very hot.

## UNIT 11 RECORDING 7

T = Tim    I = Interviewer
I:  So Tim ... you live in Rio de Janeiro in Brazil. There are a lot of beaches there. In fact, there are a lot of beautiful beaches in many parts of Brazil.
T:  Yes.
I:  What about holidays? Do you stay in Brazil for your holidays?
T:  Yes, I stay in Brazil ... but I always leave Rio. I like going to a quiet place when I go on holiday. The beach in Rio is very busy!
I:  So, where did you go for your last holiday?
T:  I went to a beach in the northeast of Brazil ... a really quiet, beautiful place in the state of Ceará.
I:  Mm ... nice ... and when did you go there?
T:  I went in February last year. It was really nice.
I:  And ... who did you go with?
T:  I went with my family ... my wife and two children.
I:  Two children?
T:  Yes.
I:  And how did you travel?
T:  Well, the journey was quite difficult. It took a long time. First, we went by plane ... from Rio to Fortaleza. That took about three or four hours.
I:  Ooh ... that's a long time!
T:  Yes, Brazil is very big!
I:  Yes!
T:  Then, we went by bus to a small town and after that, we got a different bus to the beach. We were very tired when we got there but it's really beautiful there.
I:  Where did you stay?
T:  We stayed in a small hotel ... very small ... with only a few rooms ... really near the beach ...
I:  So what did you do there?
T:  Well, nothing really! I mean, we went to the beach and swam in the sea and we ate out in small restaurants ... delicious food. We ate a lot of delicious fish.
I:  Did you enjoy your holiday?
T:  Yes, it was fantastic! We loved it! In fact, I'd like to go back ...

## UNIT 12 RECORDING 1

S = Sarah    T = Tom
S:  OK ... so let's talk about our summer holiday. What do you want to do?
T:  Summer holiday? Oh ... well, I don't want to go anywhere really. I want to stay here and play football.
S:  What? What do you mean? Stay here?
T:  Yes, I want to stay here and play football with my friends ... with the team.
S:  But I want to travel ... go somewhere exciting ... maybe go diving or something.
T:  But ... well, that's very expensive ... and anyway, I want a cat and then we need to be here ... to look after the cat.
S:  A cat? Why? I mean ... really?
T:  Yes, I like cats and I want to get a cat ... or maybe two cats.

S:  But we can't just stay here and look after the cat! That's really boring! I want to have some fun! I don't want to get a cat! I don't like cats ... and anyway, I want to travel round the world ... with you.
T:  Well ... I'm not sure about that. I don't want to travel. I don't want a holiday. It's expensive ... as I said ... and I want to buy a house with you. I don't want to spend money on travelling ... you know ...

## UNIT 12 RECORDING 2

1  A:  What do you want to do?
   B:  I want to take part in a run for charity.
2  A:  Do you want to perform on stage?
   B:  No, I don't. I want to learn to play the guitar for myself.
3  A:  What does he want?
   B:  He wants a bike. He wants to cycle to work every day.
4  A:  Does she want to do a course?
   B:  Yes, she does. She wants to learn Spanish, but she doesn't want to do an exam.

## UNIT 12 RECORDING 6

1  A:  What are you going to do this weekend?
   B:  I'm going to visit friends.
2  A:  Are you going to have a holiday this year?
   B:  Yes, I'm going to stay with my sister in the USA.
3  A:  What are you going to do after class?
   B:  I'm going to have lunch.
4  A:  Are you going to go out this evening?
   B:  No, I'm going to stay in and watch TV.

## UNIT 12 RECORDING 9

1  A:  What colour is the T-shirt?
   B:  It's green and blue.
   A:  What size is it?
   B:  I think it's small.
2  A:  What colour is the jacket?
   B:  It's red and black.
   A:  What size is it?
   B:  I think it's extra-large.
3  A:  What colour are the umbrellas?
   B:  They're pink and grey.

# Irregular verb list

| VERB | PAST SIMPLE | PAST PARTICIPLE |
| --- | --- | --- |
| be | was/were | been |
| beat | beat | beaten |
| become | became | become |
| begin | began | begun |
| bend | bent | bent |
| bite | bit | bitten |
| blow | blew | blown |
| break | broke | broken |
| bring | brought | brought |
| build | built | built |
| burn | burned/burnt | burned/burnt |
| burst | burst | burst |
| buy | bought | bought |
| can | could | been able |
| catch | caught | caught |
| choose | chose | chosen |
| come | came | come |
| cost | cost | cost |
| cut | cut | cut |
| dig | dug | dug |
| do | did | done |
| draw | drew | drawn |
| dream | dreamed/dreamt | dreamed/dreamt |
| drink | drank | drunk |
| drive | drove | driven |
| eat | ate | eaten |
| fall | fell | fallen |
| feed | fed | fed |
| feel | felt | felt |
| fight | fought | fought |
| find | found | found |
| fly | flew | flown |
| forget | forgot | forgotten |
| forgive | forgave | forgiven |
| freeze | froze | frozen |
| get | got | got |
| give | gave | given |
| go | went | gone/been |
| grow | grew | grown |
| hang | hanged/hung | hanged/hung |
| have | had | had |
| hear | heard | heard |
| hide | hid | hidden |
| hit | hit | hit |
| hold | held | held |
| hurt | hurt | hurt |
| keep | kept | kept |
| kneel | knelt | knelt |
| know | knew | known |
| lay | laid | laid |
| lead | led | led |
| learn | learned/learnt | learned/learnt |

| VERB | PAST SIMPLE | PAST PARTICIPLE |
| --- | --- | --- |
| leave | left | left |
| lend | lent | lent |
| let | let | let |
| lie | lay | lain |
| light | lit | lit |
| lose | lost | lost |
| make | made | made |
| mean | meant | meant |
| meet | met | met |
| must | had to | had to |
| pay | paid | paid |
| put | put | put |
| read | read | read |
| ride | rode | ridden |
| ring | rang | rung |
| rise | rose | risen |
| run | ran | run |
| say | said | said |
| see | saw | seen |
| sell | sold | sold |
| send | sent | sent |
| set | set | set |
| shake | shook | shaken |
| shine | shone | shone |
| shoot | shot | shot |
| show | showed | shown |
| shut | shut | shut |
| sing | sang | sung |
| sink | sank | sunk |
| sit | sat | sat |
| sleep | slept | slept |
| slide | slid | slid |
| smell | smelled/smelt | smelled/smelt |
| speak | spoke | spoken |
| spend | spent | spent |
| spill | spilled/spilt | spilled/spilt |
| spoil | spoiled/spoilt | spoiled/spoilt |
| stand | stood | stood |
| steal | stole | stolen |
| stick | stuck | stuck |
| swim | swam | swum |
| take | took | taken |
| teach | taught | taught |
| tear | tore | torn |
| tell | told | told |
| think | thought | thought |
| throw | threw | thrown |
| understand | understood | understood |
| wake | woke | woken |
| wear | wore | worn |
| win | won | won |
| write | wrote | written |

**Pearson Education Limited**
Edinburgh Gate
Harlow
Essex CM20 2JE
England
and Associated Companies throughout the world.

www.pearsonelt.com

First published 2014
ISBN: 978-1-447936947
Set in Bliss Light 10.5/12pt
Printed in Slovakia by Neografia

**Acknowledgements**
The Publisher and authors would like to thank the following people and
institutions for their feedback and comments during the development of
the material:

Nicola Perry, Surrey, UK; Emily Bell, Southport, UK; Lisa Phillips,
IH Buenos Aires, Argentina; Chris Rogers, Cardiff, UK; Agnieszka
Tyszkiewicz-Zora, University of Lodz, Poland; Elizabeth Gregson,
University of Trento, Verona, Italy

**Photo acknowledgements**
The Publisher would like to thank the following for their kind
permission to reproduce their photographs:

(Key: b-bottom; c-centre; l-left; r-right; t-top)

**Alamy Images:** Jeronimo Alba 35t, Bill Bachmann 66bl, Caro 83b,
ColsTravel 53c, Sally Cooke 20c, David Davis Photoproductions
RF 20t, Mike Goldwater 21b, Hangon Media Works Private limited
36-37c, Hemis 53tl, LJSphotography 97bl, Chris Pancewicz 52t, Peter
Phipp / Travelshots.com 85b, Prisma Bildagentur AG 64tl, Robert
Harding Picture Library Ltd 84l, Dan Santillo NZ 53tr; **Corbis:** Sergei
Bachlakov / Xinhua Press 67t, Heide Benser 7t, Sam Bloomberg-
Rissman / Blend Images 44bl, Paul Burns / Tetra Images 39b, Tim
Clayton 70 (Rafael Nadal), Bruno Cortes / Demotix 66br, John
Dowland / PhotoAlto 94, van Eick / dpa 17 (Vanessa Amorosi), Jose
Fuste Raga 33c, Blaine Harrington III 20b, Rainer Holz 57, JGI / Blend
Images 78, Juice Images 6br, Philippe Lissac 89t, John Lund / Sam
Diephuis / Blend Images 35c, Lucy Nicholson / Reuters 17 (Domnina
and Maxim Shabalin ), Ocean 6t, 96b, Albert Olive / epa 17 (Lionel
Messi ), Celia Peterson / arabianEye 64r (inset), Photosindia 44br,
SuperStock 80t, Per Winbladh 18, Jean-Yves Ruszniewski / TempSport
66l, 68cr; **DK Images:** 16tl (flag), 24-25 (Fruit), 51tr, 53 (Kiwi bird),
59tl, Gerard Brown 48 (dog), Terry Carter 14c, Brian Delf 53 (map),
Tim Draper 39t, Ian O'Leary 49 (chocolates), 93 (box of chocolates),
William Reavell 24-25 (Sushi ), William Shaw 47c, Mark Thomas 14tl,
Matthew Ward 88l, 93 (flowers), Stuart West 48 (Turkish lamb and
pomegranate pilaf); **Fotolia.com:** Africa Studio 93 (beautiful silver
earrings), 93 (shopping bag), aigarsr 41bl, amenic181 24-25 (Coffee ),
anjelagr 89b, Subbotina Anna 58c, ARTENS 88bl, auremar 50br, Kitch
Bain 71 (Cricket bat), bakerjim 24 (B), bmaki 93 (polka dot mug),
Ionescu Bogdan 76-77 (Pen and Ink), Chris Brignell 24 (G), riccardo
bruni 18 (Eva), CCat82 84-85c, Eky Chan 32-33 (background), Cmon
18bl, **CURAphotography** 85, Delphimages 61l (Buddha & orchid),
**denio109** 24-25 (Ice cream and fruit), doris_bredow 48 (Music Score ),
**eelnosiva** 24 (I), elen_studio 16tr, Elenathewise 59br, **EpicStockMedia**
36, ExQuisine 50-51c, felinda 93 (scarf), Fotofermer 24 (E), Freesurf
45 (background), 96-97 (background), gjp311 97br, godfer 76-77
(dressmakers dummy), goodluz 18 (Tim), Maksym Gorpenyuk 18b,
**Marius Graf** 49 (Popcorn), Grafvision 24-25 (Sea Bream), Ronald
Hudson 8/6, IFelix 14bc, JackF 48 (girl), **jamirae** 49 (Box of tissues),
JJAVA 24-25 (Spaghetti), Kablonk Micro 8/1, khunaspix 76-77
(architecture plans), Jules Kitano 14cl, Patryk Kosmider 83r, Kzenon
26, luminastock 31b, Olga Lyubkin 37t, M.Rosenwirth 85t, mangostock
50tr, mediagram 63bl, **michaeljung** 43t, miklyxa13 9t, Minerva
Studio 8/2, 8/8, 16bl, Monkey Business 23t, **monticellllo** 24 (L), 49
(mineral water), Sergii Moscaliuk 24 (H), Olga Nayashkova 76-77
(background), nerthuz 76-77 (Movie Director Chair), **Neyro** 24 (C),
Nitr 50bl, nyul 51tl, Tyler Olson 55bl, oriori 24 (J), Natalya Osipova 42
(background), 75 (red background), Ana Blazic Pavlovic 36-37 (inset),
pekkic 40, peshkova 58tr, picsfive 29, 63br, Pixel Embargo 93 (Retro
style camera), Pixeltheater 41br, Mariano Pozo Ruiz 47tl, radub85 63tl,
**Rido** 42t, Andres Rodriguez 59tr, scaliger 41t, **Ruslan Semichev** 24

(K), Serp 71 (roller skates), **silvionka** 61r (fan), sombatnoo 93 (Puple
Polo Shirt), Nikolai Sorokin 41c, Alexey Stiop 51tc, stockcreations
84-85b, **StockPhotosArt** 24 (F), Swapan 71 (Cricket ball ), teressa 58cl,
verdateo 68b, Viktor 24/D, 24-25 (Assorted ice cream - background
image), **volff** 24 (A), WimL 93 (Christmas Gifts), **yahyaikiz** 27t,
Alexander Yakovlev 58l, yamix 72l, 76-77 (ballet shoes), yuriyzhuravov
50l, 56, yurkaimmortal 80l, 81, alexandre zveiger 36t; **Getty Images:**
15 (Adele), 17 (Jessie J), 33t, 70 (Daniel Craig), 70 (Shakira ), 70-71,
72c, Peter Adams 86b, Lori Adamski Peek 82, AFP 15 (Neymar),
15 (Vladimir Putin), 69l, Bloomberg 18tl, Cultura / Julian Love 27r,
FilmMagic 17 (Sandra Bullock ), 70 (Harper Seven), fotostorm 34,
Hulton Archive 69r, 72tl, lethang photography 83t, moodboard 51
(Ruthie), SambaPhoto / Alexandre Wittboldt 85c, Betsie Van der Meer
8/4, Washington Post 72tr, WireImage 70 (Priyanka Chopra), 74;
**Imagemore Co.,** Ltd: 16tr (flag), 63tr; **John Foxx Images:** Imagestate
46l; **MIXA Co., Ltd:** 71 (dog); Pearson Education Ltd: Gareth Boden
87, Jules Selmes 8/5; **PhotoDisc:** C Squared Studios 71 ( teddy bear);
**Photolibrary.com:** Hill Street Studios. Nicole Goddard 18 (Ben),
Mike Kemp 55t; **Photoshot Holdings Limited:** 77t; **Plainpicture Ltd:**
apply pictures 47br, Fancy Images 51 (John), 95, Hexx 22tr, Johner
47tr, photocake.de 47bl, Thomas Reutter 89c, Kniel Synnatzschke
64l (inset); **Press Association Images:** Maurizio Gambarini / AP 15
(Lang Lang), Frank Gunn / The Canadian Press 15 (Oprah Winfrey),
Silvia Izquierdo / AP 18tr, John Shearer / Invision 15, Marcio Jose
Sanchez / AP 15 (Stephanie Rice), Dennis Van Tine / ABACA USA /
Empics Entertainment 73, Ian West / PA Wire 18br; **Reuters:** Siphiwe
Sibeko 66tr; **Rex Features:** 68tl, Paul Brown 66tl, Glenn Copus /
Evening Standard 70 (Nelson Mandela), Fotobank 75t, Peter Heimsath
68bl, Image Source 49tr, Kazden 17 (Javier Bardem), Alex Lentati /
Associated Newspapers 75b; **Shutterstock.com:** arek_malang 61tr,
auremar 44tr, Christian Bertrand 88br, bikeriderlondon 6bl, Carlos
Caetano 50tl, Orhan Cam 64tr, Hung Chung Chih 14cr, Hluboki Dzianis
93 (background), fengzheng 36l, 38b, hiroshitoyoda 55cr, imagedb.com
11br, iofoto 50r, V. J. Matthew 67 (maple leaf ), Kamira 38t, Kedsirin 9,
kosmos111 44tl, LDprod 48, Pius Lee 14l, legenda 55br, leungchopan
16tl, Eugenio Marongiu 42l, 44cl, matka_Wariatka 71l, Jeanne McRight
11bl, Dudarev Mikhail 46r, ostill 10, PeterSVETphoto 28l, pio3 22tl,
Nevena Radonja 6l, Olga Reutska 48 (boy), Rihardzz 58cr, Adrin
Shamsudin 44cr, Shots Studio 55cl, ssuaphotos 86t, Studio Intra 12,
TalyaPhoto 16br, TonyV3112 19tr, 54t, Max Topchii 58tl, warmer 19b,
Cedric Weber 19br, 20l, Tracy Whiteside 86tr, Otna Ydur 8/7, Olena
Zaskochenko 96t, Zurijeta 23b; **Sozaijiten:** 88t; **SuperStock:** age
fotostock 31t, Don Paulson Photography / Purestock 11r, 19r, 25r, 33r,
41r, 47r, 55, 63, 71, 77, 85r, 93r, Fancy Collection 37b, Salva Garrigues
/ age fotostock 21t, Glow Images 13b, Image Source 60-61c, JTB Photo
33b, Juice Images 65, Robert Harding Picture Library 32t, 32c, Tips
Images 60tl, Travel Library Limited 32b; **www.imagesource.com:** 16bl
(flag), 16br (flag), HBSS 8/3

**Cover image:** Front: **SuperStock:** Don Paulson Photography /
Purestock

All other images © Pearson Education

Every effort has been made to trace the copyright holders and we
apologise in advance for any unintentional omissions. We would be
pleased to insert the appropriate acknowledgement in any subsequent
edition of this publication.

**Illustrated by**: Nathalie Dion (AGM) pp7, pp21, pp79; Andrew Lyons
(Handsome Frank) pp30, pp90-91; Peskimo (Synergy Art) pp22, pp28-
29, pp32, p42, pp46, pp74, pp80, pp84, pp90, pp92, pp96, pp97